Managing
Land
Use

ENVIRONMENT AT RISK

Managing
Land
Use

REBECCA STEFOFF

Marshall Cavendish
Benchmark
New York

Published by Marshall Cavendish Benchmark
An imprint of Marshall Cavendish Corporation

Other Marshall Cavendish Offices:
Marshall Cavendish International (Asia) Private Limited, 1 New Industrial Road, Singapore 536196 • Marshall Cavendish International (Thailand) Co Ltd. 253 Asoke, 12th Flr, Sukhumvit 21 Road, Klongtoey Nua, Wattana, Bangkok 10110, Thailand • Marshall Cavendish (Malaysia) Sdn Bhd, Times Subang, Lot 46, Subang Hi-Tech Industrial Park, Batu Tiga, 40000 Shah Alam, Selangor Darul Ehsan, Malaysia

Marshall Cavendish is a trademark of Times Publishing Limited

All websites were available and accurate when this book was sent to press.

Library of Congress Cataloging-in-Publication Data

Stefoff, Rebecca, 1951–
Managing land use / Rebecca Stefoff.
p. cm. — (Environment at risk)
Includes bibliographical references and index.
Summary: "Provides comprehensive information on land management, its importance, and the environmental threats placed upon it"—Provided by publisher.
ISBN 978-1-60870-478-1 (print) ISBN 978-1-60879-675-4 (ebook)
1. Land use—Juvenile literature. 2. Land use—Environmental aspects—Juvenile literature. 3. Land use—United States—Juvenile literature. 4. Land use—Environmental aspects—United States—Juvenile literature.
I. Title.
HD156.S74 2012
333.73' 130973—dc22
2010035818

Editor: Christine Florie
Publisher: Michelle Bisson
Art Director: Anahid Hamparian
Series Designer: Sonia Chaghatzbanian

Expert Reader: Mark W. Anderson, Coordinator, Ecology and Environmental Sciences Program, The University of Maine, Orono

Photo research by Marybeth Kavanagh
Cover photo by *First Light/Alamy*
The photographs in this book are used by permission and through the courtesy of: *SuperStock*: Stock Connection, 2-3, 5, 65; age fotostock, 20, 82-83; Robert Harding Picture Library, 27, 28; All Canada Photos, 37; *Cutcaster*: Robert Adrian Hillman, 1, 2, 10-11, 16-17, 26, 38-39, 66-67; *The Image Works*: Thor Swift, 6, 54; Andre Jenny, 19; Sean Ramsay, 31; UNEP/Still Pictures, 42; Michael Siluk, 56; The Natural History Museum, 72; National Aeronautics & Space Administration/SSPL, 74; *Getty Images*: David McNew, 13; Dorling Kindersley, 24; NASA/Science Faction, 34; Bill O'Leary/The Washington Post, 59; Melissa Farlow/National Geographic, 62; Stephen Alvarez/National Geographic, 67; *Alamy*: imagebroker, 15; Rick Dalton-Ag, 35; Tom Uhlman, 46; *Photo Researchers, Inc.*: Gary Hincks, 30; Pasquale Sorrentino, 76; *AP Photo*: Mark Lennihan, 43; *Newscom*: HO/AFP/Getty Images, 80

Printed in Malaysia (T)
1 3 5 6 4 2

Contents

One
This Land Is Whose Land?

In 2010 the *Wisconsin State Journal* reported a battle brewing in Perry, a small rural town in Dane County, in the southern part of the state. The conflict concerned the land around a historic church. At the heart of the matter was a more general question: who has the right to decide how land will be used?

The answer may seem simple. In the United States, "[t]he property owner is the primary land use decision maker," wrote one scholar of land law in 2004. In practice, however, land use questions are often extremely complicated, whether they involve a small country church or a vast expanse of wilderness. In disputes over land use, the property owner may not be the only decision maker, or the final one.

Land use issues involve many interested parties, including property owners, the government, civic bodies, developers, and activists. In Fresno, California (left), prime farmland has been sold off to accommodate suburban housing.

Property Rights and Preservation in Perry

As many as a thousand people each year visit Perry's historic building, the Hauge Log Church. Dating from 1852, the church was the first built in western Wisconsin by the Norwegian Lutherans who settled the area. In 1974, in recognition of its significance, the National Park Service placed the Hauge Log Church on the National Register of Historic Places, a list of sites within the United States that deserve to be preserved, usually through a combination of government and private funds.

Preservation of the church, however, raised another issue: what would happen to the privately owned land around the church? The outcome was a tug-of-war between preservationists, who wanted to keep the land undeveloped as a setting for the church, and supporters of property rights, who viewed the preservationists as land grabbers.

The conflict started in 2000, when a man who owned land next to the historic church attempted to build a house and a barn on his property. Townspeople complained that the house and barn would lessen the appeal of the church, interfering with the scenic vistas of rolling farmland that form the building's setting. In 2001 the town's governing board responded to the citizens' concerns by declaring that 33 acres (13.4 hectares) of land around the church formed a "historic district," to be developed into a park.

That land, however, was privately owned. To buy it, the board raised money from state and county grants and from donations. With these funds the town was able to buy almost two-thirds of the land within the newly identified historic district. Unfortunately for the town's plans, the owner of 13 acres—the man who had planned to build the house and barn—refused to sell. In 2008 the town finally acquired his 13 acres through eminent domain, which is the right of government (federal, state, or local) to purchase a citizen's property without regard to the citizen's wish to sell.

When the town of Perry used eminent domain to acquire those 13 acres, it offered to pay the owner $74,000. The man went to court to dispute the amount, and in 2009 a jury awarded him $312,500, an amount that is almost the town's entire yearly budget. Payment was put on hold while the court decided how much the town should also pay toward the lawyers' fees.

Meanwhile, the 33-acre parcel of land around the church had sparked another dispute. Perry's town board does not have the authority to pass zoning ordinances, the laws that define how particular pieces of land may be used. The town therefore asked the zoning committee of Dane County's governing board to designate the 33 acres as an official county historic district. This would make it easier for the county to block development around the church in the future. It might also pave the way for the entire district to be added to the National Register of Historic Places.

Legal recognition of the historic district would "create a sense of place in perpetuity," explains a member of the Perry town board, meaning that the character of the land around the church would remain unchanged into the future. One historian with the National Register says that although "the boundaries selected for a National Register property are [generally] confined to the limits of that historic property," there are exceptions. Another National Register historian suggests that the town could argue that the views are what make the site historic. A Wisconsin architecture writer points out that development has become a problem around many historic sites, such as Civil War battlefields. In his opinion, "you do want to prevent what's happening," and the county historic district sounds like a good idea.

Not everyone agrees. One member of local government calls the proposed historic district "an abuse of power by Dane County." A spokesperson for an association of real estate brokers argues that "there is nothing in the state or county guidelines that makes this property historic" and says that the town of Perry and Dane County are using "a zoning weapon" against property rights.

Everyone agrees that the Hauge Log Church is a historic site worthy of protection. How far, though, should that protection extend? Was it right for community residents to keep a

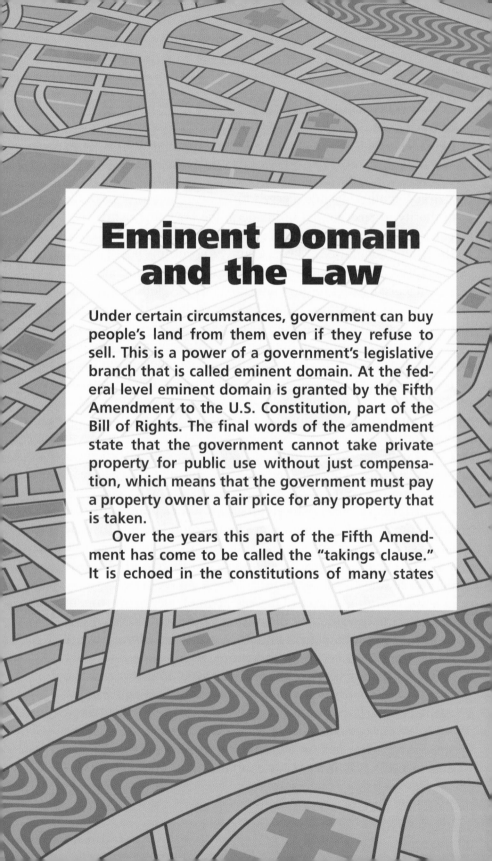

Eminent Domain and the Law

Under certain circumstances, government can buy people's land from them even if they refuse to sell. This is a power of a government's legislative branch that is called eminent domain. At the federal level eminent domain is granted by the Fifth Amendment to the U.S. Constitution, part of the Bill of Rights. The final words of the amendment state that the government cannot take private property for public use without just compensation, which means that the government must pay a property owner a fair price for any property that is taken.

Over the years this part of the Fifth Amendment has come to be called the "takings clause." It is echoed in the constitutions of many states and communities. These laws give federal, state, or local governments the right to require a land-owner to sell property even if the landowner does not want to sell. However, property acquired in this way must be devoted to public or civic use, either by the government directly or by an organization appointed by the government. If, for example, owners refuse to sell land that a government wants to use for highway construction or urban redevelopment, the government can invoke the power of eminent domain to take the land, paying the owner what it considers to be fair market value.

Thousands of court decisions at both the state and federal levels have found eminent domain to be constitutional. It is well established as law and as one of government's necessary powers. Individual claims of eminent domain, however, frequently lead to emotional debates about property rights and land use—and to more court cases.

man from building a house and barn on land he owned near the church? Should the landowner have been allowed to build on his own land, even if it changed people's impressions of the old church? The dilemma of the Perry historic district is repeated every day around the world, in large cases and small ones, as people clash over the question of how land should be used, and who gets to decide.

Stakeholders

Questions or disputes about land use have stakeholders—individuals or groups with some stake in the outcome. Many land use issues are enmeshed in a web of multiple stakeholders. Typical stakeholders include the following:

Private property owners, especially neighbors

Government at any or all levels

Local civic bodies such as neighborhood associations and business groups

Developers, investors, bankers, and others with financial interests in the property or its future use

Organizations that promote various interests, such as wildlife conservation, recreation, resource use (mining, for example), or environmental protection

Activists who become directly involved and work to rally support for or against certain outcomes

Home ownership is a simple illustration of the stakeholder concept. Along with the rights of ownership come certain responsibilities. Homeowners must usually pay property taxes to cities, towns, or counties. They are also required to follow a number of local, state, and federal regulations, such as building and zoning codes, restrictions against eliminating wetlands, rules against burying hazardous or toxic materials on private property, and public nuisance laws that prevent people from, for example, using their yards as trash dumps. The owner is

In 2006 demonstrators in Los Angeles, California, were handcuffed after being arrested during a protest sparked by the eviction of urban farmers from land whose owner wanted to build a warehouse.

13

the primary stakeholder in decisions about how to use his or her property, but government bodies, environmentalists, and neighbors are stakeholders as well.

In the United States, federal and state regulations apply to some aspects of land use. Many everyday land use issues, however are governed by the local jurisdiction, whether it is a city, county, township, or municipality.

The city of Portland, Oregon, for example, has enacted many rules to protect urban trees and increase tree canopy, which is the total amount of tree coverage within the city. Trees provide shade, help clean the air, and are highly valued by many Portlanders for aesthetic reasons—in other words, they like the way the city looks with a lot of trees. Trees that grow on parking strips, between sidewalks, and along streets are covered by these rules, and so are some trees on private property. "Tree wars" occasionally break out in the city's neighborhoods when property owners want to cut down trees that other people think should be left alone, and people have been known to take to the streets to block tree-cutting equipment and wood chippers. A disagreement over a single tree may involve many stakeholders: the property owner, the owner's neighbors or community association, local environmental activists, and the Urban Forestry Division or another city agency that enforces tree regulations.

Ownership and Control

"Not all land is 'owned,'" writes Rutherford Platt, an expert in land use law. "Around the world, and in more traditional societies within the United States, land and the resources associated with it are held in some form of *common tenure*, that is, held by a cluster of families, a tribe, a village, or some other social group." Each society, however, has developed methods of regulating how people use the land, whether for building homes and businesses, cultivating crops, grazing livestock, or harvesting natural resources such as timber and minerals. Some of these methods are informal—use of the land is guided by custom, tradition, and "the way we do things." Other methods, like the rules of land tenure and zoning in the

The city of Portland, Oregon, protects its urban greenery through rules that affect some trees on private property.

United States, are highly structured, recognized by the state, and enforceable by law.

Land Tenure

Land tenure, or people's rights with regard to land, can take many forms. The Food and Agriculture Organization (FAO) of the United Nations groups land rights into three categories: transfer, control, and use rights.

Transfer rights include the right to sell or mortgage the property, to give it to others, and to pass it to descendants through inheritance. Holders of transfer rights may exercise

15

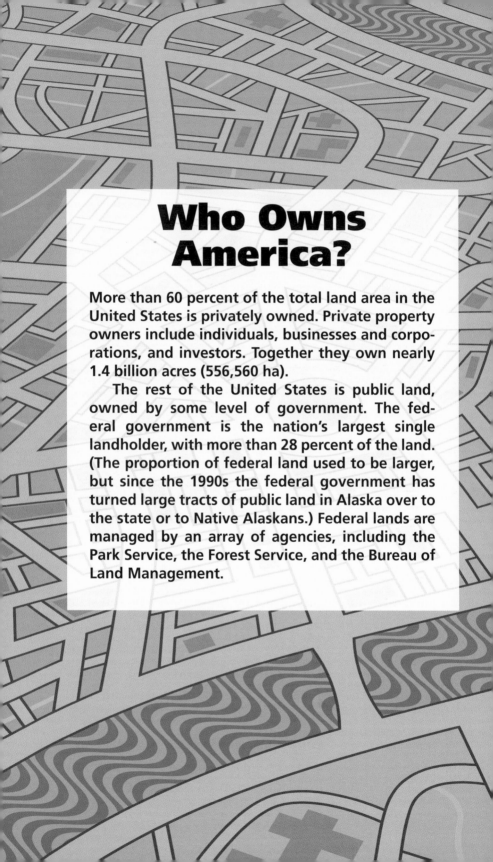

Who Owns America?

More than 60 percent of the total land area in the United States is privately owned. Private property owners include individuals, businesses and corporations, and investors. Together they own nearly 1.4 billion acres (556,560 ha).

The rest of the United States is public land, owned by some level of government. The federal government is the nation's largest single landholder, with more than 28 percent of the land. (The proportion of federal land used to be larger, but since the 1990s the federal government has turned large tracts of public land in Alaska over to the state or to Native Alaskans.) Federal lands are managed by an array of agencies, including the Park Service, the Forest Service, and the Bureau of Land Management.

Another 9 percent of the country's land belongs to state and local governments. The remaining 2 percent consists of Indian trust lands, the collectively owned reservations and other properties that are allotted to Native Americans and managed by the Bureau of Indian Affairs.

The American West has the greatest amount of federal land. Forty-one percent of all federal land is in the mountain states, 37 percent is in Alaska, and 14 percent is in the Pacific states. The other 9 percent of federal land is scattered across the eastern, midwestern, and southern states. While the U.S. government owns just 0.4 percent each of Rhode Island and Connecticut, and 0.8 percent of Iowa, it owns more than 57 percent of Utah, 69 percent of Alaska, and a whopping 84.5 percent of Nevada. Huge tracts of the West, in other words, are off-limits to private ownership. Looked at another way, however, those lands belong to all Americans.

the other types of rights to the land, which are control rights and use rights, or they may assign those rights to others.

Control rights include the right to decide how the land is used and to benefit financially from its use. Use rights are much more limited. In many countries, for example, the poorer members of agricultural communities are allowed to grow crops to feed their families, to raise a few chickens or graze a few animals, and to gather fallen wood—all on property that is owned and controlled by others.

Property rights can also be divided into four types of access:

Private, owned by an individual or group

Communal, shared by the members of a
    specific community

Open access, owned by no one, able to be used by all

State or public, owned by some level of government

Within the United States, public lands such as national parks and state forests are owned by the government but can be used by all, within the limits defined by the government. Anyone can hike in a national forest, in other words; but cutting timber there requires a lease from the proper federal agency. Another example of blended rights is the privately developed subdivision, sometimes called a "gated community." Lots and houses within such a subdivision are privately owned by individuals; but the residents share communal rights to such features as tennis courts, clubhouses, and swimming pools, and no one outside the community can claim those rights. Combinations of various rights, both formally and informally, have given rise to a wide variety of land tenure arrangements around the world.

Zoning

State, county, and local governments in the United States regulate land use through zoning, which means designating

In the United States, the federal government owns national parks that are available to be used by all.

how people can and cannot use property within various zones, or districts, of a community. Many other countries have similar land use systems.

Depending upon the size and type of the community, zoning regulations may be fairly simple or mind-bogglingly complex. At a minimum, zoning specifies what types of uses are acceptable on each parcel of land. A lot may be zoned for residential, agricultural, commercial, or industrial use, for example, or for more than one potential use. In contrast, the zoning codes of New York City and other metropolitan areas with high population density go into elaborate detail about such things as the permitted height of roofs, the amount of landscaped or paved surface that is allowed or required, and the ratio of parking spaces to residential or office units.

Zoning codes for urban areas, such as New York City, regulate building height, ratio of parking spaces to residential units, as well as the amount of landscaped and paved areas.

The idea behind zoning is that similar kinds of land use should be grouped together, so that one type of use does not interfere with another. Zoning prevents homes from being sprinkled among industrial factories, for example, or office buildings from being plopped down in the middle of farmland. In reality, however, zoning can be quite flexible. Local governments may choose to lift or alter zoning restrictions to accomplish goals such as attracting new businesses, protecting wetlands, or encouraging development in run-down districts.

Individuals or corporations can ask zoning authorities for exceptions, called variances, to the zoning rules for a particular property. Additionally, zoning codes have been challenged in court. Although courts occasionally overturn certain specific rules, the overall tendency is to rule that zoning is a constitutional and appropriate tool of city and town planning. The legal basis for zoning is the government's right and responsibility to protect the public health, safety, and general welfare, as the nation's courts have repeatedly recognized.

Land use laws are artificial, human creations. They are designed to help people, communities, and governments sort out their often-competing claims to the land. Such claims, however, are rooted in a physical reality—the ground beneath our feet. How we use the land, and whether we are successful or unsuccessful in our use of it, often depends on the nature of the land itself.

Two

Down to Basics: Soil, Landforms, and Water

Ancient warlords built their fortresses on hilltops so that they could see their enemies coming and defend themselves. Modern millionaires build mansions on hilltops to enjoy the view. In each case, the shape of the land has determined how people use it.

Topography, the scientific term for the shape of a landscape, is just one factor that affects land use. Water is another. Early cities, for example, arose in places with access to drinking water. Many were located on the shores of rivers or oceans that served as highways for transportation and trade.

The most basic factor in land use, though, is soil, the stuff of which land is made. Many types of soil exist, each with its own properties, which can make the difference between success and failure of a contemplated land use. When people build on land or cultivate it without considering the soil type, they are taking their chances.

22

The Soil Beneath Our Feet

"To understand the natural processes of the land, and to plan land use in accord with them," writes a professor of environmental planning, "there is no more fundamental place to start than the soil." Whether it is called dirt, earth, or even mud, soil is the foundation for every use of the land.

Soil is made up of inorganic minerals mixed with organic material from decaying plants and animals. Soil also contains some air, as well as water that holds dissolved nutrients, such as nitrogen. Variations in the sizes and proportions of these ingredients create a wide range of soil types.

The organic, nutrient-rich part of soil is found in the upper layer, called topsoil. Soil's mineral structure, however, comes from the underlying rock. Over time, rock breaks down into particles because of weathering. The process of weathering can be physical, as when temperature changes cause rock to expand, contract, and split. Or it can be chemical, as when water dissolves minerals as it flows through cracks in the rock, changing the composition of the rock. Most soil results from both physical and chemical weathering.

Weathering produces mineral particles, but mineral particles alone do not make soil. Organic matter such as earthworm droppings and decaying leaves also form part of soil's upper layer. Because conditions across Earth's surface are highly variable, soil forms at various rates—but always slowly. It takes from one hundred to four hundred years for natural processes to create 0.39 inches (1 centimeter) of soil.

Pedologists, or soil scientists, classify the mineral particles produced by weathering according to their size. Cobbles—small rocks and pebbles—are larger than gravel. Sand particles are smaller than gravel, but still large enough that air and water can move freely through the pores, or spaces between particles. Silt is similar to sand, but smaller and finer, with smaller pores. The smallest and finest soil particles are clay, which has very small pores between the particles. Clay is sticky when wet because the particles swell with water and adhere to one another.

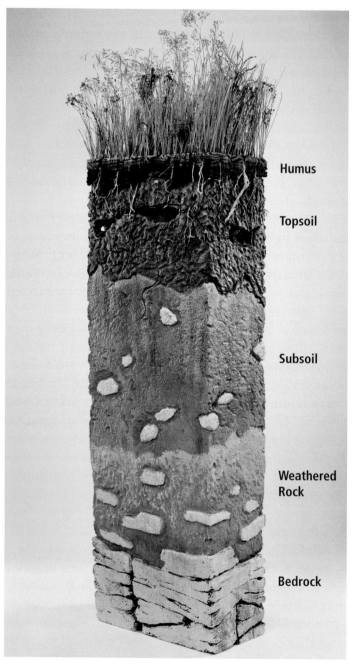

Humus

Topsoil

Subsoil

Weathered
Rock

Bedrock

Soil covers much of the land on Earth. It is made up of layers:
humus, topsoil, subsoil, weathered rock, and bedrock.

These broad categories can be divided into many subtypes, with different classification systems for different kinds of land use. In the case of farming, for example, the U.S. Department of Agriculture defines twelve soil types by their ratios of clay, sand, and silt. Clay is hard for plant roots to penetrate, sand does not hold water and nutrients well, but silt is suitable for growing crops. When planners consider the construction of buildings or highways, however, they use the Unified Soil Classification System, which divides soil into fifteen categories based on factors such as drainage, slippage, and the ability to bear weight.

The Shape of the Land

Earth's soil is not distributed evenly across a world of smooth landscapes. The planet's underlying rock surface forms mountains, rifts, and basins. Soil particles travel across this uneven surface, carried by many forces. Rivers and glaciers move pebbles, rocks, and boulders. Winds and streams carry sediment, which consists of loose particles of silt, sand, or dry clay.

All these materials are deposited into a variety of landforms, including sand dunes in deserts, deltas at river mouths, barrier islands along seacoasts, and talus cones (piles of loose soil and rock) at the base of cliffs or steep slopes. The volume of soil shifted by natural forces can be enormous, as the people of eastern Australia saw in September 2009, when a combination of drought and high winds produced a massive dust storm—a cloud of reddish airborne sediment that measured 310 miles by 620 miles. The storm deposited much of the sediment in the Pacific Ocean off Australia's coast.

The shape of the land often helps determine how it is used. A flat plain, for example, is an easier place to farm than a steep mountain slope—but if the slope has fertile soil, people can grow crops on it by creating terraces, small flat fields built up by packing soil behind a series of stone walls. Land use planners can evaluate the shape of the land by using the same tool that well-prepared hikers carry: a topographic map. Topography refers to measuring and mapping the contours of the land's surface. A topographic map, or topo, uses marks called

How to Analyze Soil

You don't need a science lab to do basic soil analysis. Dig a hole, scoop out an undisturbed shovelful of soil, then analyze it by following these steps from the federal government's Soil Science Basics website.

To start, examine a ped—one of the units in which your particular soil naturally occurs. If the soil is very dry and sandy, the ped may be a single grain. If the soil is wet and clayey, the ped may be a heavy clod. Between those extremes, peds may occur as small lumps like cookie crumbs, or chunks, sheets, or columns.

Moisten some soil slightly with water from a spray bottle, working the water through the sample. Rub a small amount of the damp soil between your thumb and forefinger. Sand feels gritty. Silt feels soft, like flour. Clay feels sticky. Many soils are made of up of two types of particles, but one type usually predominates.

If your sample feels both gritty and moist, and if you can easily form it into a loose ball and then crush the ball, you might have loam, a type of soil that is about 40 percent silt, 40 percent sand, and 20 percent clay. Try planting something—many experts consider loam ideal for gardening and farming.

A huge amount of sand and sediment engulfed eastern Australia in 2009. The city and harbor of Sydney were affected by the red dust storm.

contour lines to indicate the direction, steepness, and height of every slope.

Water Matters

The presence (or absence) of water affects how people use land. In turn, land use can have a significant effect on water. One example of this two-way influence is groundwater, which exists in large underground natural reservoirs called aquifers. A plentiful supply of groundwater that can be drawn to the surface in wells is an asset for both agriculture and urban growth.

Farmers in China terrace their sloping fields to grow rice.

Human use of the land above the aquifer, however, may pollute the groundwater with agricultural chemicals such as fertilizer and pesticides, while overuse drains the aquifer faster than natural processes can restore it.

Aquifers fill with groundwater as part of the hydrologic cycle, which is "the continuous movement of water on, above, and below the surface of the Earth." Through the hydrologic cycle, also called the water cycle, water interacts constantly with land. At various points in the cycle, water can be a liquid, a vapor, or a solid (ice). It falls from the atmosphere onto land in the form of precipitation—rain and snow. Once water has fallen onto land, it may evaporate back into the atmosphere, infiltrate (seep into the soil), or run off along the surface until it flows into a stream, river, lake, or ocean. Hydrology is the study of these processes.

Topography determines how surface water will drain from a particular area of land. As a result of factors such as hills, valleys, and slopes, drainage occurs in natural patterns known as watersheds (sometimes called catchment basins). Within a watershed, all water drains ultimately into the same body of water. Small watersheds are contained within larger ones. A valley with a tiny creek trickling along its floor is a small, local watershed; the valley on the other side of the hill, with its own creek, is a separate watershed. On a larger scale, the Mississippi River watershed covers most of the United States east of the Continental Divide, an imaginary line that runs along the crest of the Rocky Mountains.

Certain types of watersheds require special attention from land managers and land use planners. These include watersheds in areas undergoing land development, watersheds that are prone to flooding, and watersheds that contain (or may contain in the future) reservoirs storing water for human use.

Another hydrologic feature of concern in land use planning is the wetland, a low-lying area where the soil is saturated with water at least part of the time. The pools, lakes, and marshes of wetlands provide critical nesting and feeding habitats for birds and other wildlife. Land use laws in many places prohibit the destruction of wetlands; alternatively,

This illustration depicts the drainage of a river into a drainage basin. It includes smaller rivers and streams and lakes that drain into a main river before reaching the sea.

developers may be required to create new wetlands or restore damaged ones.

Soil and the City

Soil isn't just for farms and gardens. It's everywhere, including towns and cities. Urban soil, however, often suffers from serious problems.

Impervious surfaces, which cannot be penetrated by water, are one problem. Every time a building is constructed or a street or parking lot is paved, that piece of land becomes impervious. Water cannot infiltrate the soil, so it pools and flows, creating puddles. When the drainage capacity of urban streams and storm drains is overloaded, during big storms or heavy rains, large-scale street flooding can occur.

Compaction is another problem. It happens when weight—even the weight of pedestrians walking along park paths—presses on soil, making it dense. Compacted soil drains poorly and prevents the growth of plant roots. Soil that is heavily compacted may act like an impervious surface and contribute to runoff and flooding.

Erosion or soil loss is a major concern, and not just in cities. When land development removes the natural vegetation cover, soil becomes vulnerable. It may dry out and be carried away on the wind, or it may be washed into streambeds by rain. Significant erosion on slopes can lead to mudslides, landslides, and the collapse of structures.

When soil erodes, major destruction can occur, as can be seen here. The backyards of these cliff homes have fallen into the sea in Pacifica, California.

Certain types of land use create the problem of soil contamination. Urban brownfields—abandoned or neglected industrial and commercial areas within cities—often have soil that contains the residue of waste dumping, fertilizer, pesticides, pollution carried in runoff water, and chemical spills. Expensive soil cleanup is needed before these areas can be redeveloped and made useful once again.

Land use is shaped by the interaction of soil, topography, and water, together with human development. With proper understanding of these factors and their interactions, planners and developers may be more likely to use the land wisely. Failure to achieve and act on such understanding, whether in cities or in the countryside, can have grim consequences.

Three
Misusing, Overusing, and Abusing the Land

The resources of the land are vitally important to the human race. The land supports food crops and forests. It contains minerals. The surface of the land, where we live, build our cities, and work, is a resource, too—one that may become increasingly valuable as the world grows more crowded with people, all of whom require living space.

Oceans and other bodies of water cover nearly 71 percent of Earth's surface. The remaining 29 percent of the world is land. About 10.5 percent of that land is arable, which means that it can be used for growing crops that must be regularly replanted, such as wheat, corn, and rice. Permanent crops, such as fruit and nut trees and coffee bushes, are grown on another 1 percent of the land. Approximately 88 percent of Earth's land surface either is unusable (ice, deserts, mountain ranges) or is covered by forests, pastureland, and human constructions such as cities, roads, and factories.

A study published in 2008, using satellite images from 2000, reported that at the beginning of the twenty-first century 22 percent of Earth's ice-free land surface was being used

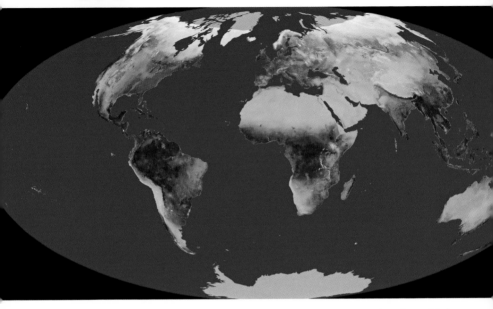

A 2007 satellite image of Earth illustrates the land areas that have high amounts of vegetation (dark green) and those that do not.

as pastureland, and 12 percent was used for growing crops. "On balance," said one of the study's authors, "the percentage of agricultural land looks set to increase."

Clearly, the human race must produce food, and people need places to live and work. Human needs, however, create pressure on the land. Population growth contributes to pressure—the more people there are, the more food and living space are needed. Technology can also be a source of pressure. For example, oil pipelines, which were first used in the late nineteenth century, allow people to send oil and natural gas over long distances more cheaply than the same fuels could be shipped by train. In addition, pipelines can carry the fuels through areas without railways. The technological advance of the pipeline brought new environmental problems, however, in the form of hundreds of spills, fires, and explosions along pipelines in many parts of the world.

Social changes can also bring new pressures to bear on the land. Between 1900 and 2000, for example, the United States changed from a rural nation to an urban one. In 1900 slightly more than 60 percent of Americans lived in the country or in small towns, while slightly fewer than 40 percent lived in cities. By 2000 the balance had shifted: the U.S. population was 79 percent urban and 21 percent rural.

With the shift from rural to urban came changes in land use. Fewer people worked the land, yet they produced ever greater amounts of food by using new tools such as tractors, fertilizers, and pesticides, and advanced irrigation techniques. The shift to large-scale farming of a single crop, or monoculture, led to the rise of industrial agriculture. Intensive farming sometimes caused erosion, exhaustion of the nutrients in the soil (known as soil depletion), and the spread of pollution in the form of runoff from the fields. At the same time, as cities expanded to house their growing populations, extensive tracts of land were paved and developed.

Industrial agriculture arose to meet the need for increased food production as population grew and a rural nation became an urban one.

Land Degradation

When land is overused, or used inefficiently or shortsightedly, the result can be land degradation:

> Land degradation, a decline in land quality caused by human activities, has been a major global issue during the 20th century and will remain high on the international agenda in the 21st century. The importance of land degradation among global issues is enhanced because of its impact on world food security and quality of the environment. High population density is not necessarily related to land degradation; it is what a population does to the land that determines the extent of degradation. People can be a major asset in reversing a trend towards degradation. However, they need to be healthy and politically and economically motivated to care for the land, as subsistence agriculture, poverty, and illiteracy can be important causes of land and environmental degradation.

Degraded land becomes less productive or usable. Degradation can have many causes. One is erosion, the loss of soil through the action of wind or water. According to one estimate, worldwide soil loss due to erosion totals 75 billion tons a year. Three other major causes of land degradation are deforestation, desertification, and pollution.

Deforestation

If forests are cut down and not replaced by natural growth or tree planting, forested land becomes nonforested land, a result called deforestation. Human-caused deforestation occurs when forests are harvested for timber or cleared so that land can be used for crops, pasture, and building sites. Forest fires, destructive insects, and climate change also contribute to deforestation.

Forests currently cover about 9.8 billion acres (4 billion ha), or 31 percent of Earth's land area, according to the

Deforestation not only affects the land, it has negative impacts on the environment.

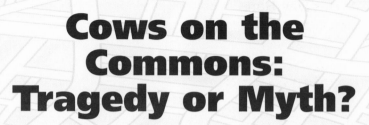

Cows on the Commons: Tragedy or Myth?

When many people use a resource but none of them owns it, what happens to the resource? In 1968 American ecologist Garrett Hardin answered that question in an influential and controversial article called "The Tragedy of the Commons."

Hardin's primary theme in "The Tragedy of the Commons" was the need to control the growth of the human population. He touched on topics ranging from parking meters and pollution to national parks and shopping malls. In each case, Hardin argued that individuals satisfy their own needs even when doing so is destructive to society.

The best-known example from Hardin's article involves "the commons"—a type of land use in which a piece of pasture is the common, or shared, property of a village or community. Everyone's cows can graze on the commons. For each cow that grazes, there is a benefit: nourishment to the cow, which will ultimately produce milk or meat. But each cow also damages the commons, trampling the soil, polluting the area with manure, and reducing the total available grass. Because all the benefit goes to the individual cow owners, while the damage is spread out among everyone who uses the commons, it is in each cow owner's best interest to graze more cows on the commons.

In this way, Hardin claimed, people will overuse or abuse a shared resource until its value is gone:

> Therein is the tragedy. Each man is locked into a system that compels him to increase his herd without limit—in a world that is limited. Ruin is the destination toward which all men rush, each pursuing his own best interest in a society that believes in the freedom of the commons. Freedom in a commons brings ruin to all.

"The Tragedy of the Commons" has influenced environmentalists and policymakers who support laws and regulations to protect common resources such as air, water, and public land. At the same time, critics have pointed out flaws in Hardin's argument, even going so far as to call the "tragedy of the commons" a myth. According to some historians who have studied traditional land use practices, many communities have effectively managed the use of shared land through peer pressure or local councils.

Whether Hardin was right or wrong about the commons, his point was that individuals cannot be counted on to limit their own use of shared land, even when overuse of the land hurts everyone. Was he right about this central issue? Not everyone agrees with Hardin. Even those who do agree hold differing ideas about how best to protect our common resources. The practice of grazing cows on a commons may be disappearing from much of the modern world, but the debate over "The Tragedy of the Commons" lives on.

United Nations Food and Agriculture Organization. Based on a review of 233 countries, the FAO reported in 2010 that the world had lost more than 32 million acres (13 million ha) of forest each year since 2000. Total deforestation during the decade amounted to an area about the size of the Central American nation of Costa Rica.

Bad as that sounds, it has been worse. During the 1990s about 39.5 million acres (16 million ha) of land were deforested each year. One reason the rate of deforestation has slowed is that some nations, including China, Vietnam, the United States, and India, have carried out large-scale programs of reforestation, which is the planting of new trees. Some of these programs, however, are scheduled to end by 2020.

Other nations have reduced the amount of forest cut each year. Brazil and Indonesia had the highest rates of deforestation in the 1990s. Brazil has gone from an average of 7 million acres (2.9 million ha) of deforestation each year to 6.4 million (2.6 million) each year since 2000, and Indonesia has gone from 4.7 million acres (1.9 million ha) to 1.2 million (0.5 million ha). At the continental level, overall rates of deforestation have decreased in Asia and remained stable in North America and Europe. Deforestation rates have increased in Africa and South America.

Deforestation affects a wide range of environmental issues, including climate change and species biodiversity. It is also directly linked to land degradation. Deforestation can degrade the land by removing the leaf cover that shades soil, as well as the root systems that hold soil in place. Forested areas hold rainwater, which percolates downward through the soil. In deforested areas, especially on hillsides and slopes, rainwater becomes runoff, which washes away topsoil and may cause flash floods.

A practice called slash-and-burn agriculture is a leading cause of deforestation in tropical and developing nations. In this form of farming, people cut forests to clear land for growing crops, pasturing livestock, or both. The fallen trees are burned, enriching the soil with charcoal and released nutrients. Often, however, a few years of use are enough to drain the soil of its nutrients, or cause it to erode. The agricultural people then move on to clear a new patch of land.

For years environmentalists criticized slash-and-burn agriculture as a wasteful practice that destroyed both forests and soil. Scientists are now finding that when practiced by indigenous forest-dwelling people who have used traditional methods for generations, this type of agriculture does not necessarily degrade the land. On a large scale, however, as when thousands of people migrate into the Amazon River basin and other tropical forests to carve out a living, slash-and-burn farming produces food in the short term but in the long term contributes to land degradation.

Desertification

Like deforestation, desertification is a change in the land's surface. It occurs when nondesert land becomes a desert, an arid place that receives very little precipitation. Deserts can be hot or cold, blanketed with sand like the Sahara or covered with low ground cover or shrubs. Desert and semidesert regions may support some grazing and even, with irrigation, some farming. Without extensive human manipulation, however, they are not productive landscapes.

Desertification turns land that is less suitable for human uses into land that is not suitable at all. It occurs when existing deserts spread and grow larger, either naturally or because of human activities. It also occurs when nondesert land in dry climates is altered by human activities, such as cutting trees for firewood, letting livestock overgraze the ground cover, or draining the groundwater through wells. These activities can create a degraded landscape, a human-made desert. Global climate change, whether caused naturally or by human activities such as burning fossil fuels, is another cause of desertification in various parts of the world.

Without vegetation, the soil of a desertified area becomes vulnerable to erosion by wind or sudden rainfall. The trampling hooves of livestock compact and harden the ground, decreasing its ability to absorb moisture and increasing runoff. As the land loses shade and ground cover, its soil temperature

Sand dunes threaten to engulf this desert oasis in the Sahel in Africa.

rises, causing water in the soil to evaporate more quickly, which in turn increases water loss even more. In addition, as water is drawn up through the soil to evaporate into the dry air, mineral salts that are normally distributed throughout many layers of soil are deposited near the surface, changing the chemical makeup of the soil—usually making it less fertile. As a result of these processes, often working together, land that was once fertile or productive becomes marginal, meaning that it barely supports human life and agriculture. Land that was once marginal, meanwhile, can become completely inhospitable through desertification.

About one-third of Earth's land surface is vulnerable to desertification. Among the areas that have already experienced extensive desertification, and are at high risk for more of it, are

North Africa, inland China and central Asia, and India, Pakistan, and Afghanistan.

Pollution

The three main causes of land pollution are contamination, solid waste disposal, and air pollution. Contamination means that sewage, chemical elements such as lead and mercury, or other hazardous or toxic materials such as petroleum products, are present in the soil. (Such materials are often present in water, too, because they can enter soil through water, and vice versa.) Industrial spills, illegal waste dumping, and legal but ineffective waste disposal cause contamination. Everyday use of pesticides and other garden or agricultural chemicals, which find their way into water and soil, also contributes to contamination.

Within the United States, seriously contaminated land may be identified as a Superfund site by the Environmental Protection Agency (EPA). Such sites are off-limits to most uses. They are eligible to be cleaned up and restored to usefulness by the EPA, which uses money from a federal fund. Some of the Superfund money has been recovered from polluters.

In March 2010 the Environmental Protection Agency declared New York's Gowanus Canal one of the nation's newest Superfund sites.

Some Superfund sites are enormous and highly dangerous. The EPA has called the Hanford site in south-central Washington State, where plutonium was produced for nuclear weapons and reactors, "one of the largest and most complex cleanup projects in the U.S." The government agency provides convincing details:

> Weapons production resulted in more than 43 million cubic yards of radioactive waste, and over 130 million cubic yards of contaminated soil and debris. Approximately 475 billion gallons of contaminated water was discharged to the soil. Some of the contaminants have made it to groundwater under the site. Over 80 square miles of groundwater is contaminated to levels above groundwater protection standards.

Other Superfund sites are much smaller. These include old city dumps, locations where businesses such as dry cleaners and wood-processing plants once used chemicals, and demolition sites at which old buildings were torn down without regard for proper disposal of dangerous materials such as asbestos and lead paint.

The EPA places the nation's most hazardous sites on the National Priorities List (NPL). As of 2010 there were 1,280 sites on the NPL. Three hundred forty-seven sites had been removed from the list, and sixty-two new sites had been proposed as additions to it.

Solid waste consists of garbage and trash from homes, businesses, and institutions such as schools and hospitals. The majority of this waste ends up in the land, either in legally operated disposal sites called landfills or as junk dumped illegally along roadsides and on neglected lots.

In 2008 Americans produced about 250 million tons of waste, not including liquid, industrial, construction, or hazardous waste. More than half of that trash and garbage came from homes and apartments. The waste consisted of food scraps, yard trimmings, paper, glass, metal, and other materials such as rubber, cloth, and wood. Paper accounted for 31 percent, or nearly a third, of the total. The EPA reports that slightly more than 54 percent of the solid waste was disposed of in landfills. A little more than 33 percent was recycled or composted. The remaining 13 percent was combusted, or burned in incinerators that produce energy from waste.

Between 1960 and 2008, the U.S. population grew by 69 percent, but Americans' waste production grew by 188 percent. The amount of waste produced for each American man, woman, and child increased from 2.7 pounds per day in 1960 to 4.5 pounds per day in 2008. The news is not all bad, however. Total waste production actually fell from 254 million tons in 2007 to 250 million tons in 2008. Recycling rates are increasing, too. About 69 percent of all solid waste was landfilled in 1990, and 16 percent was recycled or composted. By 2008 the landfills received only 54 percent, while 33 percent was recycled or composted.

Even if waste production keeps falling and recycling and composting rates keep rising, people in the United States and around the world will keep generating solid waste—tons and tons of it each day. It has to go somewhere, and choosing locations for landfills is one of the most important tasks in land management.

Landfills are lined with pressed clay or artificial materials such as plastic. The purpose of the liner is to contain leachate, the liquid formed by rainwater and other fluids present in the waste, which can absorb compounds from the waste and then trickle downward. Despite the use of liners, the soil beneath and around a landfill should be clayey, since clay seals well and drains poorly. Clayey soil helps prevent any leaked leachate from entering the surrounding earth or the groundwater.

Finally, air pollution contributes to land pollution. When the air contains toxic chemicals such as mercury and dioxin, these materials can make their way into the soil. Toxins in the soil, in turn, pollute water that drains through the soil.

Mitigation

Using the land need not mean misusing, overusing, or abusing it. At all levels—from small family gardens to city building permits to regional or national planning of large developments such as freeways, pipelines, and irrigation projects—efficient and environmentally sound land use practices can prevent degradation of the land, or keep degradation to a minimum.

An important element of land management and land use planning is mitigation, which means preventing damage, reducing its effects, or repairing it. At countless sites around the world, mitigation projects organized by the United Nations, by conservation organizations, or by governments and citizens have shown that land degradation can be turned around.

The former Fernald Feed Materials Production Center in Ohio processed uranium for nuclear weapons from 1951 to 1989. Today, the restored site is a nature preserve.

Case History: Fighting the Creeping Desert

One African farmer's fight against desertification became a model for others in his community. Serigne Samb's small farm consisted of plots of inherited land around his village in the northwestern part of the West African nation of Senegal. The region, which receives less than 12 inches (300 millimeters) of rainfall each year, is home to roving groups of herdspeople and their livestock as well as to settled farmers, most of whom grow crops and keep livestock of their own.

Samb's small holding suffered from problems experienced across the Sahel, the vast expanse of semiarid land that stretches across a number of African nations south of the Sahara Desert. Trees disappeared at a rapid rate, browsed by livestock or cut down to provide wood for building and also for burning to produce charcoal, a major fuel source for the people of the region. The loss of tree cover worsened the wind's erosion of the dry, sandy soil. It also reduced the amount of wood and charcoal available for human use, and of vegetation for livestock to eat. Many farmers in the area no longer grew a variety of crops for their own use; instead, they cultivated peanuts to sell. This shift to monoculture left the land more exposed than it was when the vegetation had consisted of a variety of plants, including shrubs and trees. The result: still more erosion. In short, Samb's farm—like the land occupied by many thousands of people across the Sahel—was turning into desert.

Hoping to reverse this trend, Samb applied traditional land use practices, employing farming methods that had been known in the area for generations but had fallen out of use in his time. With technical advice and some financial help from UN agencies in Senegal, Samb enclosed one of his plots—a 25-acre (10-ha) field—inside a living fence, which he created by planting trees and shrubs around the edge of the field. Samb used *Euphorbia*, a genus of plants that grazing animals generally avoid because the plants are toxic to them. This live fence prevented grazing and reduced erosion, so that trees and other vegetation could regrow on the protected plot.

At the start of the project there were fewer than a hundred trees on the plot. Twelve years later there were about 12,500. The trees and other vegetation protected by the fence were a source of wood, charcoal, fodder (livestock feed), and fruit. The Samb family not only used these products but found a source of income in selling the surplus to people in the community. The project—planting a live fence to enclose a plot, then letting the plot regrow its natural cover of mixed trees, shrubs, and plants—halted desertification and also brought clear economic benefits. Samb's success inspired others in the area to copy his methods.

Case History: Reforesting Himalayan Hills

The Shiwalik hills, in northern India's Haryana state, are foothills of the Himalayas, Asia's largest mountain range. Like other areas in and around the Himalayas, the Shiwalik hills are losing their forests. The deforestation has two main causes. First, people harvest trees—often on public land where forests are supposed to be protected—to use the wood. Second, people graze their livestock in the forests. Uncontrolled grazing prevents the forest from regrowing and also strips away the grass and other vegetation, resulting in "severe soil erosion in the hills."

One approach to the problem is provided by the Hill Resource Management Society (HRMS), an organization that lets local people participate in managing the forest resources. An HRMS branch is based in the community, and all adults are eligible to join it. Through the HRMS, local people interact with the government agencies that are responsible for land and resource control. The HRMS and the government must agree on trade-offs; that is, if people agree not to abuse the forest resources, their needs must be met in other ways. The goal is to make forest use sustainable, which means that although people use the resource, they do not overuse it. Usage is limited to a level at which the forest can sustain itself through regrowth.

With funds from the government of India and the Ford Foundation, the United Nations and an Indian research institute launched a pilot HRMS program in an area of sixty-five villages scattered over 49,400 acres (20,000 ha) of rugged, degraded land in the Shiwalik hills. The goal was protection of the watersheds through conservation of forests and soil. Villagers were asked to reduce their use of the state-owned forests in exchange for new supplies of irrigation water that would help them cultivate other, nonforest land. The Forest Department built new dams to provide the irrigation water, while the HRMS became responsible for maintaining the dams and water channels. As the irrigated land became more productive, pressure on the forests decreased.

The government offered other incentives, or benefits, to encourage people to become involved in HRMS. One incentive was leasing parcels of forest land and pastureland to the HRMS, whose members could use these designated parcels in return for halting their uncontrolled use of other forest areas. Another incentive was leasing commercial fodder to the HRMS at affordable rates. The HRMS also gained permission to increase the harvest from local bamboo forests in return for managing the forests and preventing fires.

Within five years there were twenty-seven HRMS branches in the program area. Members of these groups policed the use of local resources. Illegal grazing and tree cutting were reduced, and so was soil erosion. Degraded areas became revegetated. At the same time, the people served by HRMS experienced economic benefits. Access to more fodder boosted the milk production from livestock, supporting a growing dairy industry. With regular sources of wood and fodder, household incomes increased. The Forest Department benefited, too, as the task of managing the state-owned forests was now shared by the villagers. The program succeeded because the local people who had been abusing public land were recognized as stakeholders. Once they were given a say in managing the forest, they became willing to use it under self-policed guidelines, giving the forest a better chance at long-term survival.

Case History: Restoring a Wetland

In the United States, one of the most serious forms of land degradation involves wetlands, which may be covered with shallow water for all or part of the year. These marshes, swamps, bogs, and coastal zones provide many benefits. They absorb rainfall, which helps prevent floods. They purify water, absorbing sediment and fertilizer as these materials cycle through the soil. Wetlands are also vital habitat and feeding grounds for many species of birds, animals, and water life.

In the 1600s, when Europeans began settling North America, the area that is now the lower forty-eight states had about 220 million acres of wetlands. Since that time more than half of those wetlands have been drained or built over as people have turned the land to other uses. Agriculture and construction have been the main reasons for the loss or degradation of wetlands, although climate change is also drying out some once-wet areas. In the mid–1970s the rate of wetland loss in the United States began to slow. Scientists, governments, planners, and communities recognized the importance of wetlands, and new laws and policies were put in place to conserve these important resources. Although wetlands are still being lost, some have been restored through mitigation projects.

In Morgan County, Alabama, a 657-acre tract of land along Flint Creek was once a wooded wetland. Years ago the trees were cut, and the land was drained and turned into a cattle and grain farm. Beginning in 1998, however, the land was turned back into a wetland through a process called mitigation banking.

Mitigation banking means creating, restoring, or preserving a natural area such as a wetland in order to balance the environmental damage that can be expected from nearby development. Federal, state, and local governments give developers credits for mitigation projects that have been successfully completed. The developers, in turn, can "cash in" these credits when they plan future developments. Selecting and creating a mitigation site calls for cooperation between a number of public and private interests, including the U.S. Army Corps of Engineers (which must approve the site), the federal Environmental Protection Agency and the Fish and Wildlife Service, local soil and water conservation boards, landowners, developers, and environmental consulting firms.

Restoration of the Flint Creek wetland involved planting 160,000 native trees such as bald cypress, river birch, and oak. Then the site was monitored for five years to see whether the restoration would be successful. It was. The former farmland became a new wildlife habitat, and the amount of soil that washed from it into the creek fell from 15 tons of sediment per acre each year to less than one ton. Another benefit of the mitigation is that the wetland, which now belongs to and is managed by the county, has become "an outdoor conservation classroom for area students."

Four

The Human and
Natural Landscapes

"**Land is always** transforming itself," urban planner and professor David C. Soule wrote in 2006. He pointed out that landscape features such as meadows, forests, water channels, and habitat change naturally. "However," he continued, "the human settlement pattern often radically, and usually permanently, changes undeveloped land to developed land."

Ever since humans started digging pit houses and constructing stick huts back in the dawn of prehistory, people have built things on the landscape. When they began herding animals, planting crops, and trampling out paths and roads, they continued this process of change, which in time led to the modern world of twelve-lane highways, towering skyscrapers, and suburbs that stretch to the horizon.

At the same time, however, human beings care, sometimes passionately, about the natural world. In the words of American biologist Edward O. Wilson:

> In the United States and Canada more people visit zoos and aquariums than attend all professional athletic events combined. They crowd the national

parks to view natural landscapes, looking from the tops of prominences out across rugged terrain for a glimpse of tumbling water and animals living free. They travel long distances to stroll along the seashore, for reasons they can't put into words.

The natural world has the power to stir our feelings of curiosity, relaxation, and awe. Even as the human race continues to multiply across the globe, building, using resources, and changing the face of the world, many individuals and societies work to protect and preserve natural landscapes, wildlife, and ecosystems. The modern conservation and environmental movements have produced, among other things, the American system of national parks and wildlife refuges.

Human needs—water, food, shelter, employment, transportation—determine how people use the land. One challenge of land use in the United States and around the world is balancing human needs and conservation, seeking harmony between the human and natural landscapes. Another challenge is learning how to build and live in a world full of natural hazards and disasters.

People and Land Use in America

During the second half of the twentieth century, two factors reshaped the human landscape of the United States. One was population growth, and the other was the rise of the suburb.

Between 1950 and 2000 the nation's population rose from 151 million people to 281 million—an increase of 86 percent. Growth didn't stop there, of course. The U.S. Census Bureau reported in 2010 that the country's population had reached more than 310 million (out of a total world population of 6.9 billion). Demographers—people who research population statistics and trends—predict that the U.S. population will reach 438 million by 2050.

Along with the explosive growth of the American population between 1950 and 2000 came a major change in the way people lived. The United States was already becoming an urban, rather than a rural, nation. The shift to urbanization continued in the decades after 1950, but those decades introduced a new type of urban life—one based in the suburbs. These were settled areas, many of them newly developed, outside the more densely built-up centers of cities. Unlike urban cores, where many people lived in apartments, rowhouses or townhouses, or shared buildings such as condominiums, the suburbs consisted of single-family houses on private lots, usually with grass lawns.

It was the automobile that allowed people to move to the suburbs even when they continued to work in the central cities. Land use expert John Randolph writes, "Massive highway construction and the rise of the automobile as the primary mode of personal transportation freed people to flee the crime and grime of the city and find personal space in the suburbs."

Suburbs, in other words, were created by land use decisions, especially the federal government's decision to make highways the center of the nation's transportation plan.

As the American population boomed, so did the growth of suburbs, large tracts of land developed with many homes.

Today many land use planners see the continuing spread of suburbs—usually referred to as "sprawl"—as a problem that should be solved. Others believe that the suburbs are here to stay, because people want them, but that they can be more efficiently designed. Architects, environmentalists, and planners from both sides of the debate are creating new approaches to land use in urban centers as well as outlying areas. These approaches offer alternatives for future development.

Suburbia: Sprawling Nightmare or American Dream?

Former Maryland governor Parris N. Glendening cites the following reasons for viewing the expanding suburbs as unwelcome sprawl:

> In its path, sprawl consumes thousands of acres of forests and farmland, woodlands and wetland. It requires government to spend millions extra to build new schools, new streets, new water and sewer lines. . . . In its wake, sprawl leaves boarded up houses, vacant storefronts, closed businesses, abandoned and often contaminated industrial sites, and traffic congestion stretching miles from urban centers.

There are many reasons to disapprove of suburban expansion. Because traditional suburbs are designed for drivers, not pedestrians or cyclists, and because they are usually located some distance from stores, parks, and workplaces, sprawl makes people dependent on automobiles to get to and from the suburbs. Dependency on cars creates long commutes for workers, leading to traffic gridlock on urban and suburban highways. It also increases gasoline consumption and the resulting air pollution. In addition, suburbs drain the resources of municipalties, which must keep extending services into new areas rather than improving the infrastructure in older communities. Finally, by attracting middle-class and upper-middle-class people who can afford suburban life, the suburbs reduce the social, economic, and cultural diversity of urban cores. City centers are left to the poor and, in the desirable neighborhoods of cities such as New York and Los Angeles, the very rich.

Another argument against suburban expansion focuses on the loss of farmland:

> Much of the land being consumed by sprawl is prime farmland lost to food production forever. . . . Developers favor farmland because it tends to be relatively flat or gently sloping and cleared. . . . Sprawl threatens the future of farming in America. Over half of the fruit, vegetable, and dairy producing farmland faces development pressure. . . . Pennsylvania lost 20 percent of its farmland between 1969 and 1992. . . . As prime agricultural lands are lost to sprawl, less suitable land for farming must be brought into cultivation, which often require more chemicals or irrigation, both of which create further environmental problems.

Farmland still exists next to a suburb in St. Charles, Minnesota—but for how long?

Many communities have taken steps to reverse the flight to the suburbs, or at least to slow it down. One of the first to take serious steps in this direction was Portland, Oregon, which in 1980 enacted an Urban Growth Boundary "to protect farms and forests from urban sprawl and to promote the efficient use of land, public facilities and services inside the boundary." The Urban Growth Boundary was a line drawn between urban and rural land. Development and growth would be concentrated inside the boundary, in the urban district. The surrounding rural district—the site of many flourishing farms, orchards, plant nurseries, and wineries—would remain rural. In this way Portland hoped to prevent limitless suburban sprawl.

One goal of the Urban Growth Boundary was infill, which means filling the existing city with denser population and development rather than expanding outward. Portland introduced zoning rules and tax benefits to encourage smaller-than-usual private lots, multistory homes and apartment buildings, condominiums, and multifamily residences.

Urban planner and historian Joel Kotkin thinks that projects like the Urban Growth Boundary are ultimately doomed. "Attempts to halt suburbanization, such as those in Portland, have had at best mixed results," he wrote in an article titled "In Praise of Suburbs," published in 2006. "Although widely held up as an exemplar of smart growth, Portland's tight suburban growth limits have tended to drive residents farther out and have done little to reduce the area's traffic congestion." The reality, Kotkin argues, is that city planners want people to live in dense, urban neighborhoods, but "a large percentage of people continue to seek out single-family houses." This point has been made in another way by planner and environmentalist David Soule, editor of a volume entitled *Urban Sprawl: A Comprehensive Guide*: "If sprawl is so bad, why do the majority of Americans choose this pattern of settlement?"

Many Americans simply regard the single-family house on a private lot as the ideal way to live. According to Kotkin, for example, 84 percent of adult Californians prefer that living arrangement to any other. The land use planners who will influence future development cannot afford to overlook the power of what people want.

Alternative Approaches

Partly as a reaction to suburban sprawl, planners and architects in the United States and elsewhere have come up with alternative approaches to development, such as smart growth, new urbanism, building smaller homes, wet growth, and new suburbanism.

The term "smart growth" is believed to have been coined by urban and regional planner Robert Yaro in the 1970s. The idea behind smart growth, of which Portland's Urban Growth Boundary is an example, is to prevent or limit development on open land while directing development toward cities, suburbs, and town centers that already exist. Governments can accomplish these goals through many means, including zoning rules, purchases of open land to be set aside for conservation, changes in the way federal and state funds are used for infrastructure such as road building, and rewards (tax breaks) or penalties (higher tax rates) for developers. "The smart growth movement recognizes that there must be continued development in the United States, especially of housing," writes Anthony Flint, the author of *This Land: The Battle over Sprawl and the Future of America* (2006). "The humble suggestion is that it can be better planned, designed, and distributed."

A movement that began in the early 1990s has been called the new urbanism. It promotes the creation of new communities that are planned from the start as complete, environmentally friendly neighborhoods. These communities feature sidewalks and bicycle lanes on all streets, houses on small lots with porches in front and alleys or garages in back, and services such as stores, parks, gardens, and libraries within walking distance.

New urbanism emphasizes mixed-use development. Instead of row after row of single-family houses, communities are a mix of houses, apartments, condominiums, rowhouses or townhouses, and work/home structures that combine businesses, studios, or offices with living space. One of the first of

Kentlands, in Gaithersburg, Maryland, is an example of new urbanism. The town center was designed to have an urban feel although it is part of a self-contained suburban development.

these compact, mixed-use communities was Kentlands, Maryland, described on the community website as a "neo-traditional community" and a "town within a city."

Between 1970 and 1990, land used for residences in the large cities of Chicago and Atlanta increased eight to ten times more than population increased. Why the big difference between population growth and the amount of land used for new housing? American houses, on average, kept getting bigger, even though the number of people in the average household was decreasing as family sizes got smaller.

In 2009, however, news media reported that the size of the average new home was dropping, perhaps as a result of a recession that had slowed the American economy. Although the trend toward smaller houses may not last, a small-house movement has formed, with websites and magazines about building, buying, and living in small residences. People can

59

now purchase home-building kits or plans for very small residences—some, measuring under 200 square feet in area, are called "tiny houses."

Small houses are not for everyone, but they offer affordable, compact, and private living quarters for single people, couples, elders who want to live near but not with their children, and others who like the idea of downsizing their homes. Not only are the houses smaller than traditional residences, but so are the homeowners' expenses, such as heating and electricity bills. Many communities have adopted zoning laws that permit small houses on partial lots as a way of increasing infill.

The relationship between water supply and land use is "one of the hottest topics in land use today," according to Craig Anthony Arnold, author of *Wet Growth: Should Water Law Control Land Use?* (2005). In the view of Arnold and some other planners, the availability and protection of water supplies should be a major consideration in land development. The law is already moving in that direction. In some areas, voters have approved laws stating that developers cannot receive building permits until they demonstrate that there is enough water available to supply the new development for twenty years. And in 2002 the U.S. Supreme Court ruled that the Tahoe Regional Planning Authority had the right to ban new development around scenic Lake Tahoe, located on the California–Nevada border, because the lake's water quality was endangered by "development-related runoff."

Urban development scholar Joel Kotkin predicts that the suburbs, not the central cities, will be the dominant form of American urban life in the twenty-first century. In "Toward a New Suburbanism" he writes:

> In attempting to turn back the clock, urbanists have spent a generation looking for a means to revive city centers as the core of American economic, political, and social life. Yet in seeking to build the urban future, they have largely ignored the one place that

clearly represents the predominant form of urbanism in the twenty-first century: suburbia.

The best way to tame suburban sprawl, in Kotkin's view, is not to try to get rid of suburbs—which won't work, because people like suburban living. Instead, planners should realize that suburbs are not static. They are growing, evolving, and more diverse than they used to be. Business, shopping, and cultural districts are springing up in old, formerly neglected town centers and industrial sites to serve the needs of people who live in older suburbs. Developers of newer suburbs are beginning to include bike paths, shopping districts, and parks, borrowing some ideas from the new urbanism movement.

As a result, many suburbs are becoming more like villages, or at least are closer to shopping districts, hotels and hospitals, and cultural activities than they used to be. Together with technological innovations, such as videoconferencing, that let many people work from home for at least part of the time, these developments have the potential to reduce the suburbs' negative aspects, such as traffic congestion, while preserving the space and privacy that drew people to the suburbs in the first place.

Conserving Nature and Resources

For more than a century the conservation movement has had a voice in land use in the United States. Conservation concerns are now part of land use planning and decision making in many parts of the world.

Although conservation has many meanings, in general it refers to saving, protecting, or making prudent use of nature. It is related to, or part of, the environmental movement, but conservation is less concerned with air pollution and other issues that may affect human well-being than it is with natural places, wildlife, ecosystems, and resources. Conservationists include a broad range of interests. Among them are people who want to preserve areas of untouched wilderness in a pristine state, people whose focus is protecting endangered plants

61

Activists rally against mountaintop removal for surface mining.

and animals and their habitats, and people who want to see resources such as soil and forests used responsibly so that they will not become degraded or disappear.

Conservation influenced an innovative land use decision in the United States in 1872, when Congress set aside 2 million acres in Wyoming and Montana as "a pleasuring ground for the people":

> This was Yellowstone National Park, the first national wilderness park in the world. In forming the park, Congress was influenced by the railroad companies, which had realized that extraordinary landscapes were a valuable commercial resource: Scenery would draw tourists, and tourists would buy train tickets. Yet although Yellowstone was created in large part for commercial reasons, conservation also played a role. There was a growing sense that the grandest features of the landscape—many

of which were on land still owned by the federal government, especially in the West—should be both protected from development and made available to the public.

Yellowstone paved the way for the creation of more national parks, both in the United States and in other countries. Conservation lands in the United States are now a patchwork of various kinds of protected areas, administered by a variety of federal agencies. The U.S. National Park System—which includes monuments, preserves, historic sites, rivers, seashores, recreation areas, and more in addition to national parks—consists of 393 different sites covering more than 84 million acres. The National Wildlife Refuge System, managed by the U.S. Fish and Wildlife Service, encompasses 553 sites with a total of 150 million acres, as well as 38 wetlands management districts. The Forest Service, a division of the U.S. Department of Agriculture, oversees 193 million acres of publicly owned forests and grasslands. Congress has also set aside 680 wilderness areas covering a total of more than 106 million acres in 44 states (57 million acres in Alaska alone). Hundreds of state and county parks add to the total.

These American conservation lands enjoy varying levels of protection. The building of new roads is not permitted in wilderness areas, for example; but livestock owners may graze herds in places that were used for livestock grazing before they received the wilderness area designation. National parks are protected from development or resource exploitation; but hunting, mining, and oil and gas extraction are allowed on national preserves and some other public lands. National forests are managed for timber production.

In varying degrees, the governments of many other countries have enacted laws to preserve or protect pieces of land and the wildlife and ecosystems that the land supports. The success of these efforts depends on how effectively the protection granted by law can be enforced on the land. In places that lack funds for staff and training, wild places and animals do not always receive the protection that they have been granted on paper.

Governments are not the only bodies concerned with conservation. NGOs, or nongovernmental organizations, play an active role in conservation at all levels. Local associations clean up parks and beaches. Groups such as the Audubon Society work to educate the public and lobby Congress on issues that affect the well-being of wildlife. The Nature Conservancy is an organization that makes land use decisions with its pocketbook. By using money from donations, the Nature Conservancy is able to buy environmentally important parcels of land around the world for conservation purposes. Many other international nonprofit groups, such as the Rainforest Alliance, monitor land use around the world and strive to make conservation a key element in decision making.

Land conservation is important for many reasons. Biodiversity—which is indicated by the number of species able to live on the land—is vitally dependent upon the survival of natural habitats. Conservation serves long-term human needs, too, by encouraging sustainable use of soil, forests, and other resources of the land. Beyond species counts and the dollars-and-cents wisdom of protecting useful resources, however, the natural world has value that cannot be measured. Conservation lands are important as places of recreation, renewal, and inspiration for people now and in the future.

When Human and Natural Worlds Collide

Natural occurrences such as earthquakes, landslides, wildfires, floods, and tornadoes are severe threats to human life and property. For all levels of government, one important goal of land use planning and management is hazard mitigation, which means trying to achieve "the long-term reduction of the effects of natural hazard events."

There are a number of ways to reduce the effects of natural hazards on people and their property. One of the most obvious is to move away from the hazard, but there are others.

Moving away from the hazard. This is generally impossible or impractical on a large scale—the city of San Francisco, for example, is not going to be moved to a new location, even though it has suffered several disastrous earthquakes.

Visitors observe a herd of bison in Yellowstone National Park.

Individuals and businesses, however, may choose to move away from locations that have experienced floods or other natural disasters, or are at high risk for such events.

Limiting potential damage. Planners and lawmakers can use zoning laws to prevent people from building in hazardous areas or discourage the practice through financial penalties, such as permit fees and high insurance costs. They can also use incentives such as tax benefits to encourage people to build in low-risk rather than high-risk areas. How the land in a hazardous area is used makes a difference, too. Using the land around a volcano as livestock pasturage, for example, carries less potential risk than building cities on it.

A Conservation Hotspot in the Caucasus

You've probably heard or read about the endangered Amazon rain forest of South America. You might know about the many species of lemurs and other animals threatened with extinction on the island of Madagascar, off the coast of Africa. But do you know about the environmental crisis in the Caucasus (right)?

The Caucasus is the region between the Black Sea and the Caspian Sea on Russia's southern border. Divided among the nations of Russia, Georgia, Armenia, Azerbaijan, Turkey, and Iran, this region has been identified as a biodiversity hotspot—an area that has a large number of unique species and a high degree of threat to their habitats—by the nonprofit organization Conservation International. The Caucasus is home to 1,600 species of plants that grow nowhere else on Earth, as well as two endangered species of turs, a type of mountain goat. Illegal hunting, illegal plant collecting, and clearing of the forests for fuel wood now threaten these unique plant and animal species. The natural vegetation and habitat that once covered 205,800 square miles has been reduced to 55,500 square miles in extent.

A total of 16,500 square miles of the Caucasus is under some form of conservation protection, including a network of six nature reserves and national parks in the Russian part of the region. Conservation International and other environmental and wildlife organizations are working with the nations of the Caucasus, hoping to set aside more protected areas and to improve the enforcement of existing conservation laws. Their goal is to preserve the region's record—so far, no species has gone extinct in the Caucasus.

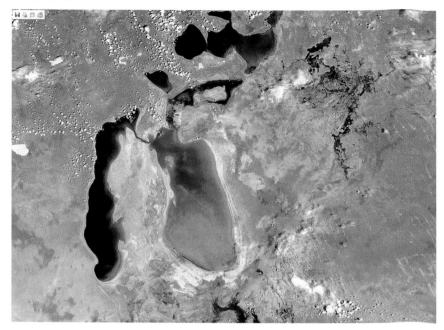

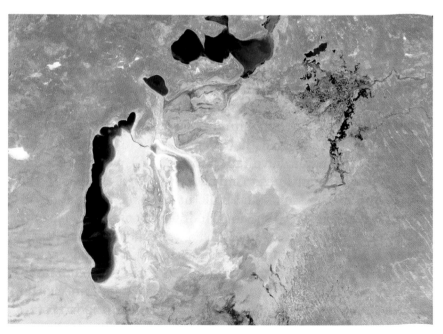

Satellite images of the Aral Sea in 2006 (top) and 2009 (bottom) show dramatic changes in the disappearing lake.

Battle for the Grand Staircase

Near the southern border of Utah is a huge staircase—a series of cliffs, separated by stretches of level ground, that rise like a miles-long flight of steps. Together with the canyons of the Escalante River, this feature of the land has given its name to a 1.9-million-acre national monument, Grand Staircase-Escalante.

Remote, rugged, and magnificent, this parcel of public land, scattered with relics of ancient Native Americans, was "the last place in the continental United States to be mapped." It is also the cause of a long-lasting land use dispute that has involved cattle rustling, controversy, and a challenge to the federal government from the state of Utah.

The Making of the Monument

The dispute over Grand Staircase-Escalanate stretches back, in a way, to 1906. That year the U.S. Congress passed the Antiquities Act, which gave presidents the power to create national monuments on federal land without a congressional review. The act was intended to allow presidents to act quickly to protect features such as Native American archaeological sites that were in danger of being looted. Since that time, presidents have created more than a hundred national monuments. Some of them, including Arizona's Grand Canyon, later became national parks with congressional approval.

Southern Utah, a land of redrock formations carved by wind, water, sand, and ice, abounds in geological wonders. Many of them, including Arches, Bryce Canyon, and Zion Canyon, had been granted protected status. Environmentalists, archaeologists, and wilderness advocates felt that the Grand Staircase-Escalante area should be protected, too. They worked for years to achieve this goal, and finally, in 1996, President Bill Clinton proclaimed the creation of the Grand Staircase-Escalante National Monument.

Lovers of redrock wilderness rejoiced. Many Utahns, however, did not share the joy. The state's governor and congressional representatives were furious—they had publicly opposed the creation of the monument and were notified of Clinton's

intention just one day before his announcement. To add insult to injury, the president
made the announcement not in Utah but
across the border in Arizona. Clinton, who
was unpopular in Utah, was in the midst of a
reelection campaign, and many accused him of
staging the announcement in Arizona to win
votes in that state. The announcement, however, was only the start of the controversy.

Redrock Rumble

The Grand Staircase-Escalante National
Monument is managed by the Bureau of Land
Management (BLM), which has had its work
cut out for it. From the start, antimonument
feeling was strong among the people of the
area, who foresaw new limits on their use of
the land. Resentment continues to simmer
among people who believe that the federal
government should not have more control
over land than the state or the people who live
and work nearby.

Ranchers had been grazing cattle on the
public land before it became a monument.
Clinton's proclamation specified that existing
grazing rights—in the form of allotments, or
permissions to use certain areas that must be
purchased from the BLM—would continue
within the monument. Since that time, however, environmental groups such as the Grand
Canyon Trust have purchased some of the
BLM grazing allotments and retired them,
aiming to reduce what they regard as ecological damage caused by cattle. By 2006 the trust
had bought up and retired about 200,000 acres'
worth of grazing allotments. Ranchers who continued to graze
cattle on allotments that had been retired were ordered to remove
their livestock from the monument. A few refused to comply.

In 1996 the Grand Staircase-Escalante in Utah was declared a national monument by President Bill Clinton, opening up controversy about who should decide how to use this land.

After the BLM removed the cattle, the ranchers "rustled" the animals away from the BLM. Area ranchers then organized and filed a lawsuit to prevent the allotments from being retired. In 2006 a federal court upheld the buyouts as legal.

Another controversy concerned the monument's mineral resources. A mining company had planned to open a coal mine on the Kaiparowits Plateau, an area enclosed by the monument. Although existing mining leases, like grazing allotments, were allowed to remain in force after the monument was created, mining operations would have to meet the environmental standards of a national monument rather than those of ordinary BLM land. Monument standards are stricter, and this caused the company to give up its lease. The mine would have created jobs and brought income to the state, and its loss infuriated many local people as well as some of Utah's elected leaders.

Still other controveries have erupted over the use of dirt roads in the monument, the BLM's ban on off-road vehicles, and the pressure by conservation activists to have part of the monument declared a wilderness area, which carries a higher level of protection. The passage of fourteen years did nothing to calm Utahns' ire over the monument—in mid–2010 a candidate for one of Utah's seats in the U.S. Senate promised that if elected he would try to get legislation passed that would limit the federal government's control over federal lands. Although legal experts regarded his proposal as unlikely to succeed, it was a sign of the deep resentment that land use decisions can create, and of the difficulty of reaching agreement on how—or even whether—to use the land and its resources.

Planning for the Future

In 1962 a British scholar of American land use described the U.S. approach to land use as a "prairie psychology," in which people believe that land is almost unlimited. Developers prepared land for use, he claimed, but did not question whether it *should* be used. Today, however, almost any proposed use of land is likely to be questioned. Citizens, neighborhoods, conservationists, business associations, environmental watch-dog groups, and government all take a keen interest in land use decisions.

The best decisions about land use are made on two levels. One level involves ownership and control: whose land is it, and who decides how it will be used? The other level concerns stewardship—meaning the responsibility to take the best possible care of something that will pass into other hands. People entrusted with making land use decisions might do well to ask, are we good stewards of the land? No matter how land is used, if it is used intelligently and thoughtfully for an appropriate purpose, it can still have value for those who will use it after us.

Notes

Chapter One

p. 7, "In 2010 the *Wisconsin State Journal* reported . . .": Matthew DeFour, "Town seeks buffer zone around historic church," *Wisconsin State Journal,* July 4, 2010, online at http://host.madison.com/wsj/news/local/article_21a72739-b1e8-5bd3-9baf-a8523e2e7e50.html. (Accessed 11/1/2010.)

p. 7, "[t]he property owner is the primary . . ." : Rutherford Platt, *Land Use and Society: Geography, Law, and Public Policy,* revised edition, Washington, DC: Island Press, 2004, p. 209.

p. 9, ". . . create a sense of place . . .": DeFour, "Town seeks buffer zone around historic church."

p. 9, ". . . the boundaries selected . . .": DeFour, "Town seeks buffer zone around historic church."

p. 9, ". . . you do want to prevent . . .": DeFour, "Town seeks buffer zone around historic church."

p. 9, ". . . an abuse of power by Dane County.": DeFour, "Town seeks buffer zone around historic church."

p. 9, ". . . there is nothing in the state . . .": DeFour, "Town seeks buffer zone around historic church."

p. 9, ". . . a zoning weapon . . .": DeFour, "Town seeks buffer zone around historic church."

p. 14, "Tree wars . . .": Janine Robben, "There's no peace in city's tree wars," *Portland Tribune,* November 23, 2003, updated October 30, 2009, online at www.portlandtribune.com/news/print_story.php?story_id = 21144. (Accessed 11/1/2010.)

p. 14, "Not all land is 'owned,' . . . ": Platt, *Land Use and Society,* p. 6.

p. 15, ". . . people's rights with regard to land . . . ": United Nations Food and Agriculture Organization, "What Is Land Tenure?" online at www.fao.org/docrep/005/y4307e/y4307e05.htm. (Accessed 11/1/2010.)

p. 16, "More than 60 percent of the total land area . . . ": U.S. Department of Agriculture Economic Research Service, "Major Uses of Land, by Class of Ownership," 2002, online at http://ers.usda.gov/publications/EIB14/eib14j.pdf. (Accessed 11/1/2010.)

p. 17, "Forty-one percent of all federal land . . . ": Major Uses of Land, by Class of Ownership."

p. 17, "While the U.S. government owns . . . ": David M. Kennedy, "Can the West Lead Us to a Better Place?" *Stanford Magazine,* May/June 2008, online at www.stanfordalumni.org/news/magazine/2008/mayjun/features/west.html. (Accessed 11/1/2010.)

Chapter Two

p. 23. "To understand the natural processes of the land. . . . ": John Randolph, *Environmental Land Use Planning,* Washington, DC: Island Press, 2004, p. 317.

p. 23, ". . . one hundred to four hundred years . . . ": Randolph, *Environmental Land Use Planning,* p. 318.

p. 25, ". . . the U.S. Department of Agriculture defines twelve soil types . . . ": U.S. Department of Agriculture, Natural Resources Conservation Service, "Soil Textural Triangle," online at http://soils.usda.gov/education/resources/lessons/texture/. (Accessed 11/1/2010.)

p. 25, ". . . divides soil into fifteen categories . . . ": Virginia Department of Transportation, "Unified Soil Classification System," online at www.occ.state.ok.us/Divisions/PST/Forms/Technical%20Forms/Orbca%20Guidance/unified%20soil%20classification.pdf. (Accessed 11/1/2010.)

p. 25, ". . . airborne sediment that measured 310 miles by 620 miles.": Bonnie Malkin, "Largest dust storms in 70 years cover Sydney," *Telegraph*, September 23, 2009, online at www.telegraph.co.uk/news/worldnews/australiaandthepacific/australia/6222210/Largest-dust-storms-in-70-years-cover-Sydney.html. (Accessed 11/1/2010.)

p. 26, ". . . federal government's Soil Science Basics website.": Goddard Space Flight Center, National Aeronautics and Space Administration, "Soil Science Basics," online at http://soil.gsfc.nasa.gov/index.html. (Accessed 11/1/2010.)

p. 29, ". . . the continuous movement of water . . . ": U.S. Geological Survey, "The Water Cycle," online at http://ga.water.usgs.gov/edu/watercycle.html. (Accessed 11/1/2010.)

Chapter Three
p. 33, ". . . bodies of water cover nearly 71 percent . . . ": Michael Pidwirny, "Introduction to the Oceans," Physical Geography, online at www.physicalgeography.net/fundamentals/8o.html. (Accessed 11/1/2010.)

p. 33, "About 10.5 percent . . . ": Central Intelligence Agency World Factbook, "Geographic Overview," updated October 26, 2010, online at www.cia.gov/library/publications/the-world-factbook/geos/xx.html. (Accessed 11/1/2010.)

p. 34, "On balance . . . ": Kate Ravilious, "Farmland is eating up the world's wildernesses," *New Scientist,* 9 February 2008, online at www.newscientist.com/article/mg19726424.800-farmland-is-eating-up-the-worlds-wildernesses.html. (Accessed 11/1/2010.)

p. 35, "In 1900 slightly more than 60 percent . . . ": U.S. Census Bureau, "Urban and Rural Population: 1900 to 1990," released 1995, online at www.census.gov/population/censusdata/urpop0090.txt. (Accessed 11/1/2010.)

p. 35, "By 2000 the balance . . . ": U.S. Department of Transportation, Federal Highway Administration, "Census 2000 Population Statistics," online at www.fhwa.dot.gov/planning/census/cps2k.htm. (Accessed 11/1/2010.)

p. 36, "Land degradation, a decline . . . ": H. Eshwaran et al., "Land Degradation: An Overview," U.S. Department of Agriculture, Natural Resources Conservation Service, 2001, online at http://soils.usda.gov/use/worldsoils/papers/land-degradation-overview.html. (Accessed 11/1/2010.)

p. 36, ". . . erosion totals 75 billion tons a year.": Eshwaran et al., "Land Degradation."

p. 36, "Forests currently cover about 9.8 billion acres . . . ": United Nations Food and Agriculture Organization, "World deforestation decreases, but remains alarming in many countries," March 25, 1010, *Global Forest Resources Assessment 2010,* online at www.fao.org/news/story/pt/item/40893/icode/en/. (Accessed 11/1/2010.)

p. 39, "Therein is the tragedy . . . ": Garrett Hardin, "The Tragedy of the Commons," *Science,* 13 December 1968, vol. 162, no. 3859, pp. 1243–1248, online at www.sciencemag.org/cgi/content/full/162/3859/1243. (Accessed 11/1/2010.)

p. 39. ". . . critics have pointed out flaws in Hardin's argument . . . ": Ian Angus, "The Myth of the Tragedy of the Commons," *Socialist Voice*, August 24, 2008, online at http://climateandcapitalism.com/?p = 513. (Accessed 11/1/2010.)

p. 40, ". . . the world had lost more than 32 million acres . . . ": "World deforestation decreases, but remains alarming in many countries."

p. 40. ". . . about 39.5 million acres . . . ": "World deforestation decreases, but remains alarming in many countries."

p. 40, "Brazil has gone from an average of 7 million acres . . . " "World deforestation decreases, but remains alarming in many countries."

p. 40, ". . . Indonesia has gone from 4.7 million acres . . . ": "World deforestation decreases, but remains alarming in many countries."

p. 40, "A practice called slash-and-burn . . . ": Jerome Taylor, "Destruction of forests in developing world 'out of control,'" *The Independent,* 14 March 2007, online at www.independent.co.uk/environment/destruction-of-forests-in-developing-world-out-of-control-440122.html. (Accessed 11/1/2010.)

p. 41, "Scientists are now finding. . . . ": "Slash-and-Burn Farming Method in Western Borneo Under Analysis," *Science Daily,* April 26, 2007, online at www.sciencedaily.com/releases/2007/04/070424180848.htm. (Accessed 11/1/2010.)

p. 42, "About one-third of Earth's land surface . . . ": Eshwaran et al., "Land Degradation."

p. 42, ". . . North Africa, inland China and central Asia . . . ": Eshwaran et al., "Land Degradation. "

p. 44, ". . . one of the largest and most complex cleanup projects . . . ": U.S. Environmental Protection Agency, Region 10 Superfund: Hanford, WA, online at http://yosemite.epa.gov/r10/cleanup.nsf/sites/hanford. (Accessed 11/1/2010.)

p. 44, "Weapons production resulted in . . . ": U.S. Environmental Protection Agency, Region 10 Superfund: Hanford, WA.

p. 44, "As of 2010 there were 1,280 sites . . . ": U.S. Environmental Protection Agency, "National Priorities List (NPL)," online at www.epa.gov/superfund/sites/query/queryhtm/npltotal.htm. (Accessed 11/2/2010.)

p. 44, ". . . Americans produced about 250 million tons of waste . . . ": U.S. Environmental Protection Agency, "Municipal Solid Waste Generation, Recycling, and Disposal in the United States: Facts and Figures for 2008," online at www.epa.gov/wastes/nonhaz/municipal/pubs/msw2008rpt.pdf. (Accessed 11/2/2010.)

p. 45, "Paper accounted for 31 percent . . . ": U.S. Environmental Protection Agency, "Municipal Solid Waste Generation, Recycling, and Disposal in the United States: Facts and Figures for 2008."

p. 45, ". . . slightly more than 54 percent of the solid waste . . . ": U.S. Environmental Protection Agency, "Municipal Solid Waste Generation, Recycling, and Disposal in the United States: Facts and Figures for 2008."

p. 45, ". . . U.S. population grew by 69 percent, but Americans' waste production grew by 188 percent.": U.S. Environmental Protection Agency, "Quantity of Municipal Solid Waste Generated and Managed," p. 2, updated March 2010, online at http://cfpub.epa.gov/eroe/index.cfm?fuseaction = detail. viewPDF&ch = 48&lShowInd = 0&subtop = 228&lv = list. listByChapter&r = 216598. (Accessed 11/2/2010.)

p. 45, ". . . from 2.7 pounds per day in 1960 to 4.5 pounds . . . ": U.S. Environmental Protection Agency, "Quantity of Municipal Solid Waste Generated and Managed," p. 2.

p. 45, ". . . from 254 million tons in 2007 to 250 million in 2008.": U.S. Environmental Protection Agency, "Quantity of Municipal Solid Waste Generated and Managed," p. 2.

p. 45, "About 69 percent of all solid waste . . . ": U.S. Environmental Protection Agency, "Quantity of Municipal Solid Waste Generated and Managed," p. 2.

p. 45, "By 2008 the landfills received only 54 percent . . . ": U.S. Environmental Protection Agency, "Quantity of Municipal Solid Waste Generated and Managed," p. 2.

p. 48, "At the start of the project there were fewer than 100 trees . . . ": United Nations Environmental Programme Success Stories, "Mr. Serigne Samb's Farm, Thiambène Till, Senegal," online at www.unep.org/desertification/successstories/10. htm. (Accessed 11/2/2010.)

p. 48, ". . . severe soil erosion in the hills.": United National Environmenal Program Success Stories, "Joint Participatory Forest Management, Shiwalik Hills, Haryana Province, India," online at www.unep.org/desertification/successstories/18. htm. (Accessed 11/2/2010.)

p. 50, ". . . the lower forty-eight states had about 220 million acres of wetlands.": U.S. Environmental Protection Agency, "Wetlands: Status and Trends," online at http://water.epa. gov/type/wetlands/vital_status.cfm. (Accessed 11/2/2010.)

p. 50 "Since that time more than half of those wetlands . . . ": U.S. Environmental Protection Agency, "Wetlands: Status and Trends."

p. 51, ". . . fell from 15 tons of sediment per acre each year . . . ": U.S. Department of Agriculture, Natural Resources

Conservation Service, "Flint Creek Wetlands Mitigation Bank Deeded to Morgan County," online at http://www.al.nrcs.usda. gov/news/sstories/06/8-06_flint_ck_wetlands_mitigation_bank-morg.html. (Accessed 11/2/2010.)

p. 51, ". . . an outdoor conservation classroom for area students.": U.S. Department of Agriculture, Natural Resources Conservation Service, "Flint Creek Wetlands Mitigation Bank Deeded to Morgan County."

Chapter Four

p. 52, "Land is always transforming itself . . . ": David C. Soule, "Defining and Managing Sprawl," in David C. Soule, editor, *Urban Sprawl: A Comprehensive Guide*, Upper Saddle River, NJ: Pearson Prentice Hall, 2006, p. 5.

p. 52, "In the United States and Canada . . . ": Edward O. Wilson, *The Diversity of Life*, New York: Norton, 1992, p. 350.

p. 53, "Between 1950 and 2000 the nation's population rose . . . ": Randolph, *Environmental Land Use Planning and Management*, p. 106.

p. 53, "The U.S. Census Bureau reported in 2010 . . . ": "US & World Population Clocks," online at www.census.gov/main/www/popclock.html. (Accessed 11/2/2010.)

p. 53 ". . . the U.S. population will reach 438 million by 2050.": Jeffrey S. Passel and D'Vera Cohn, "U.S. Population Projections: 2005–2050," Pew Research Center, February 11, 2008, online at http://pewsocialtrends.org/pubs/703/population-projections-united-states. (Accessed 11/2/2010.)

p. 54, "Massive highway construction . . . ": Randolph, *Environmental Land Use Planning and Management*, p. 106.

p. 55, "In its path, sprawl consumes . . . ": Parris N. Glendening, quoted in Soule, "Defining and Managing Sprawl," p. 3.

p. 56, "Much of the land being consumed . . . ": Sarah Gardner, "The Impact of Sprawl on the Environment and Human Health," in Soule, editor, *Urban Sprawl*, p. 242.

p. 57, ". . . to protect farms and forests from urban sprawl . . . ": Metro Regional Government, "Urban Growth Boundary," 2010, online at www.oregonmetro.gov/index.cfm/go/by.web/id = 277. (Accessed 11/2/2010.)

p. 57, "Attempts to halt suburbanization . . . ": Joel Kotkin, "In Praise of Suburbs," SFGate, January 29, 2006, online at http://articles.sfgate.com/2006-01-29/opinion/17277120_1_bay-area-suburbs-santa-cruz. (Accessed 11/2/2010.)

p. 57, ". . . a large percentage of people continue to seek out single-family houses.": Kotkin.

p. 57, "If sprawl is so bad . . . ": in Soule, "Defining and Managing Sprawl," p. 6.

p. 57, ". . . 84 percent of adult Californians prefer that living arrangement . . . ": Kotkin, "In Praise of Suburbs."

p. 58, "The term 'smart growth' is believed to have been coined . . . ": Anthony Flint, *This Land: The Battle over Sprawl and the Future of America,* Baltimore: Johns Hopkins University Press, 2006, p. 84.

p. 58, "The smart growth movement recognizes . . . ": Flint, *This Land*, p. 87.

p. 59, ". . . a 'neo-traditional community' and a 'town within a city.'": Kentlands website, online at www.kentlandsusa.com/outside_home.asp. (Accessed 11/2/2010.)

p. 59, "Between 1970 and 1990, land used for residences . . . ": Gardner, "The Impact of Sprawl on the Environment and Human Health," in Soule, editor, *Urban Sprawl*, p. 241.

p. 59, "size of the average new home was dropping. . . ": Les Christie, CNNMoney.com, August 11, 2009, online at http://money.cnn.com/2009/08/07/real_estate/shrinking_ home/?postversion = 2009081112. (Accessed 11/2/2010.)

p. 60, ". . . some, measuring under 200 square feet in area, are called 'tiny houses.'": Tumbleweed Tiny House Company, online at http://www.tumbleweedhouses.com/houses/. (Accessed 11/2/2010.)

p. 60, ". . . one of the hottest topics in land use today . . . ": Craig Anthony Arnold, *Wet Growth: Should Water Law Control Land Use?* Washington, DC: Environmental Law Institute, 2005, p. 8.

p. 60, ". . . water quality was endangered by 'development-related runoff.'": Arnold, *Wet Growth*, p. 13.

p. 60, "In attempting to turn back the clock . . . ": Joel Kotkin, "Toward a New Suburbanism," MetropolisMag.com, March 20, 2006, online at www.metropolismag.com/story/20060320/ toward-a-new-suburbanism. (Accessed 11/2/2010.)

p. 62, "This was Yellowstone . . . ": Rebecca Stefoff, *The American Environmental Movement,* New York: Facts On File, 1995, pp. 28–29.

p. 63, "The U.S. National Park System . . . ": National Park Service, "Frequently Asked Questions," online at www.nps. gov/faqs.htm. (Accessed 11/2/2010.)

p. 63, "The National Wildlife Refuge System . . . ": U.S. Fish and Wildlife Service, "National Wildlife Refuge System," online at www.fws.gov/refuges/. (Accessed 11/2/2010.)

p. 63, "The Forest Service . . . ": "Welcome to the USDA Forest Service," online at www.fs.fed.us/. (Accessed 11/2/2010.)

p. 63, "Congress has also set aside 680 wilderness areas . . . ": Bureau of Land Management, "Frequently Asked Questions: The Wilderness Idea," online at www.blm.gov/wo/st/en/prog/blm_special_areas/NLCS/wilderness2/Wilderness_FAQ.html. (Accessed 11/2/2010.)

p. 64, "the long-term reduction of the effects of natural hazard events.": Randolph, *Environmental Land Use Planning and Management*, p. 202.

p. 66, "The Caucasus is home to 1,600 species of plants that grow nowhere else . . . ": "Caucasus," Conservation International, online at www.conservation.org/explore/priority_areas/hotspots/europe_central_asia/Caucasus/Pages/default.aspx. (Accessed 11/2/2010.)

p. 66, "The natural vegetation and habitat that once covered 205,800 square miles . . . ": "Caucasus," Conservation International.

p. 68, "The disaster affected nine states . . . ": Federal Emergency Management Agency, "Buyouts Dramatically Demonstrate Avoided Flood Damage," Earthquake Engineering Research Institute Mitigation Center, Cedar Falls and Independence, IA Case Study, online at www.eeri.org/mitigation/files/resources-for-success/00016.pdf. (Accessed 11/2/2010.)

p. 68, ". . . a total cost of $4.3 million: 75 percent from federal grants . . . ": Federal Emergency Management Agency, "Buyouts Dramatically Demonstrate Avoided Flood Damage."

p. 69, ". . . buyouts would result in a savings of $6.6 million . . . ": Federal Emergency Management Agency, "Buyouts Dramatically Demonstrate Avoided Flood Damage."

Chapter Five
p. 71, "We live in the midst . . . ": Randolph, *Environmental Land Use Planning and Management*, p. 297.

p. 71, "Maps are 'graphic descriptions . . . '": Randolph, *Environmental Land Use Planning and Management*, p. 280.

p. 73, ". . . produces images resembling air photos. . . ": Randolph, *Environmental Land Use Planning and Management*, p. 288.

p. 76, "The result was a map titled . . . ": ESRI, "What Can You Do With GIS?" GIS.com: The Guide to Geographic Information Systems, online at http://www.gis.com/content/what-can-you-do-gis. (Accessed 11/2/2010.)

Chapter Six

p. 78, ". . . one of the greatest environmental catastrophes ever recorded.": "Aral Sea Loss and Cotton (ARAL Case)," December 21, 1995, online at www1.american.edu/ted/aral.htm. (Accessed 11/2/2010.)

p. 78, ". . . the lake received about 12 cubic miles of fresh water. . . ": NASA Earth Observatory, "The Shrinking Aral Sea," May 5, 2001, updated December 20, 2009, online at http://earthobservatory.nasa.gov/IOTD/view.php?id = 1396. (Accessed 11/2/2010.)

p. 79 "Environmental experts agree . . . ": "The Shrinking Aral Sea."

p. 81, ". . . the last place in the continental United States . . . ": Bureau of Land Management, online at www.blm.gov/ut/st/en/fo/grand_staircase-escalante.html. (Accessed 11/2/2010.)

p. 82, ". . . retired about 200,000 acres' worth of grazing allotments.": "Overgrazing on the Grand Staircase-Escalante National Monument," Earthjustice, June 20, 2006, online at www.earthjustice.org/our_work/victory/overgrazing_on_the_grand_staircaseescalante_national_monument.html. (Accessed 11/2/2010.)

p. 84, ". . . in mid–2010 a candidate for one of Utah's seats . . . ": Phil Taylor, "U.S. Not *'Sovereign'* Over Federal Lands, Utah GOP Senate Candidate Says," the *New York Times,* July 2, 2010, online at http://www.nytimes.com/gwire/2010/07/02/02greenwire-us-not-sovereign-over-federal-lands-utah-gop-s-30438.html?scp = 1&sq = utah % 20 eminent % 20domain&st = cse. (Accessed 11/2/2010.)

p. 84, ". . . the U.S. approach to land use as a 'prairie psychology' . . . ": John Delafons, *Land-Use Controls in the United States*, cited in Soule, "Defining and Managing Sprawl," p. 5.

Further Information

Books

Casper, Julie Kerr. *Lands: Taming the Wilds.* New York: Chelsea House, 2007.

Desonie, Dana. *Geosphere: The Land and Its Uses.* New York: Chelsea House, 2008.

Miller, Debra A. *Urban Sprawl.* Farmington Hills, MI: Greenhaven, 2009.

Morgan, Sally. *Changing Planet: What Is the Environmental Impact of Human Migration and Settlement?* New York: Crabtree, 2010.

Ruschmann, Paul, and Maryanne Nasiatka. *Private Property Rights.* New York: Chelsea House, 2007.

Geospatial Data Gateway

http://datagateway.nrcs.usda.gov/

Maintained by the Natural Resources Conservation Service of the U.S. Department of Agriculture, this site is an online catalog of geospatial information—maps and data sets—on land and resource use, the environment, and physical and human geography.

Global Land Survey

http://gls.umd.edu/

The Global Land Survey, a joint effort by NASA and the USGS, uses satellite images to create a large-scale picture of Earth. The program's goal is to measure the planet's land cover and to show how land use changed the surface of the planet between 2000 and 2010.

Globalis Interactive World Map

http://globalis.gvu.unu.edu/

Globalis is an interactive world map that uses information gathered by the United Nations and other national and international organizations to create maps that display information such as rainfall, land cover, and population density.

Guide to Geographic Information Systems

www.gis.com/

The Guide to Geographic Information Systems offers an overview of what GIS is, how it works, and how land use planners use it.

Land Policy Institute

www.landpolicy.msu.edu/

Michigan State University's Land Policy Institute promotes the study of land use, focusing on topics such as revitalizing cities and protecting soil and water resources.

Land Use/Land Cover Change
http://lcluc.umd.edu/
NASA's Land Use/Land Cover Change program tracks changes in land use and land cover worldwide. The site has links to maps and articles, such as a map of global land use hotspots.

People, Land Management, and Ecosystem Conservation
www.unu.edu/env/plec/
The People, Land Management, and Ecosystem Conservation page of the United Nations University has information about projects that team scientists with farmers to develop sustainable land use practices.

Soil Science Education
http://soil.gsfc.nasa.gov/index.html
This Soil Science Education home page is a good starting point for investigations into what soil is, how it is formed and used, and the importance of soil in agriculture and other human activities.

USAID Land Management
www.usaid.gov/our_work/agriculture/landmanagement/
The Land Management page of the U.S. Agency for International Development offers an overview of the challenges created by increasing worldwide demands on the land, with links to pages about the agency's projects in several regions.

World Resources Institute
www.wri.org
The World Resources Institute site features a number of worldwide maps related to land use, including deforestation, agricultural use, and wetlands.

Bibliography

Arnold, Craig Anthony. *Wet Growth: Should Water Law Control Land Use?* Washington, DC: Environmental Law Institute, 2005.

Babbitt, Bruce E. *Cities in the Wilderness: A New Vision of Land Use in America.* Washington, DC: Island Press, 2005.

Braimoh, Ademola K., and Paul Vlek. *Land Use and Soil Resources.* London: Springer, 2008.

Bruegmann, Robert. *Sprawl: A Compact History.* Chicago: University of Chicago Press, 2005.

DeFries, Ruth S., et al. *Ecosystems and Land Use Change.* Washington, DC: American Geophysical Union, 2004.

Diamond, Henry L., and Patrick F. Noonan. *Land Use in America.* Washington, DC: Island Press, 1996.

Entwisle, Barbara, and Paul C. Stern. *Population, Land Use, and Environment: Research Directions.* Washington, DC: National Academies Press, 2005.

Eshwaran, H., et al. "Land Degradation: An Overview." U.S. Department of Agriculture, Natural Resources Conservation Service, 2001, online at http://soils.usda.gov/use/worldsoils/papers/land-degradation-overview.html

Flint, Anthony. *This Land: The Battle over Sprawl and the Future of America.* Baltimore: Johns Hopkins University Press, 2006.

Francis, John G., and Leslie Francis. *Land Wars: The Politics of Property and Community.* Boulder, CO: Lynne Rienner Publishers, 2003.

Freyfogle, Eric T. *The Land We Share: Private Property and the Common Good.* Washington, DC: Island Press, 2003.

Hardin, Garrett. "The Tragedy of the Commons. *Science,* 13 December 1968, vol. 162, no. 3859, pp. 1243–1248, online at http://www.sciencemag.org/cgi/content/full/162/3859/124

Platt, Rutherford. *Land Use and Society: Geography, Law, and Public Policy.* Revised edition. Washington, DC: Island Press, 2004.

Plotkin, Sidney. *Keep Out: The Struggle for Land Use Control.* Berkeley: University of California Press, 1987.

Prescott, Samuel T. *Federal Land Management: Current Issues and Background.* New York: Nova Science, 2003.

Priemus, Hugo, et al. *Land Use Planning.* Northampton, MA: Edward Elgar, 2007.

Randolph, John. *Environmental Land Use Planning and Management.* Washington, DC: Island Press, 2004.

Skillen, James. *The Nation's Largest Landlord: The Bureau of Land Management in the American West.* Lawrence: University of Kansas Press, 2009.

Soule, David C., editor. *Urban Sprawl: A Comprehensive Reference Guide.* Westport, CT: Greenwood, 2006.

———. "Defining and Managing Sprawl," in Soule, David mmmC., editor. *Urban Sprawl: A Comprehensive Reference Guide.* Westport, CT: Greenwood, 2006.

Index

Page numbers in **boldface** are illustrations.

About the Author

Rebecca Stefoff is the author of many nonfiction books for young people, including the four-volume series Humans: An Evolutionary History (Marshall Cavendish Benchmark, 2010). Environmental topics she has explored in her books include ecological disasters, recycling, and extinction. In addition to works on scientific topics, Stefoff has written about social history. Information about her books for young people is available at www.rebeccastefoff.com.

It's Your Wedding —
Not Theirs

A Creative and Comprehensive Guide to
Planning a Distinctively Unique,
Personal and Sacred Celebration

By Miles O'Brien Riley, Ph. D.

Other Books by the Author:
With a Song In My Ark
The Impossible Mission
Ikthus
Getting the Good News on the Evening News
To Whom It May Concern
Gift of Love
Your Communication Plan
Training Church Leaders for TV News Interviews
Set Your House in Order
Invo's & Bene's
Tell the Truth With Kindness
Promises to Keep

AuthorHouse™
1663 Liberty Drive, Suite 200
Bloomington, IN 47403
www.authorhouse.com
Phone: 1-800-839-8640

First published by AuthorHouse 11/4/2008

ISBN: 978-1-4389-1330-8 (sc)

Library of Congress Control Number: 2008909640

Printed in the United States of America
Bloomington, Indiana
This book is printed on acid-free paper.

Book Design and Layout by Patti Appel.
Cover Photos: 13 of the 50 couples who shared wtih me their wedding wisdom and precious photos.

authorHOUSE®

vi

Virgil wrote, "Love conquers all." I agree, but only if it's wise and truthful.

cannot be with you personally to prepare for your wedding and marriage, so this book will take my place and help you make it truly YOUR Wedding—Not Theirs. Whether "theirs" refers to the powerful wedding industry, your family and friends, or that movie or TV show you watched 20 years ago. May God bless your celebration and your holy union.

After being honored to celebrate some 2000 weddings during the last 45 years, I am addressing you, My Dear Bride, primarily because I know who is doing most of the work—and the worrying. I hope this compact, practical guidebook will help you with your planning.

You will no doubt discover that organizing your wedding will be one of the most delightful and stressful and important things you will ever do. We tease brides: if you can survive the wedding, the marriage will be relatively easy.

Most of all, this book is a reminder and a plea: It's YOUR Wedding—Not Theirs! The bridal business lately has grown strong, controlling, and expensive. Wedding costs nationally are averaging $40-50,000. That's a lot to spend for a party or even a weekend. But the sobering truth is that no amount of money guarantees a great wedding. Money can't buy meaning or memories, love or class.

Syndey and Scott thank their guests

The following pages suggest tips and strategies to help you make it truly yours, an expression of your dreams, a reflection of your heart and soul-felt. Included are creative examples from 55 of my favorite brides—couples who got it and did it their way—and, now, 10 to 20 years later, have trusted me with their wedding wisdom, insightful reflections and precious photos. Hopefully, together, we will inspire you to make your once-in-a-lifetime wedding truly yours.

With blessings on your wedding and especially your marriage,

— *Fr. Miles*

PROLOGUE

My two thousand and fiftieth couple just drove off on their Harley Davidson motorcycle. Bride Cortney is a 29-year-old administrative assistant for a group of plastic surgeons and 34-year-old Mike runs a fast-growing computer sales and repair business.

Left: Bridesmaids wear comfortable "gowns"; Right: guests are welcomed to their "Aloha Wedding" with Hawaiian Leis

- They want a fun, family, Hawaiian type wedding: luau, leis, ukuleles, flip flops, sport shirts, barbecued pupus and umbrella drinks by the beach and Mother Nature's Pacific placental waters. They want a spiritual but not churchy celebration. They want it to be theirs—and not the wedding industry's.

Bride Cort and Groom Mike

- They have known each other for eight years, dated for six years and lived together for five years. I explained, non-judgmentally, that all couples in America face a 50% chance of divorce and those who live together before marriage increase the odds of divorce to 75% because co-habitation without commitment instills a loose-goosey attitude that often returns 3-7 years later when the going gets really rough. My educated suspicion (and hope) is that Cortney and Mike will be among the 25% who are successful.

- They are completely comfortable with their roles as hostess and host at their wedding (no "Barbie and Ken" "this is MY special day" "I'm so excited" "It's all about me" for these two.) They totally understand that this celebration is for all those whose love taught them how to love—and that their parents and families are their guests of honor.

- To prepare them for the integral importance of an overall theme or focus and the intimacy of love letters and personalized vows, home-made prayers and special intentions, we spent over an hour exploring my two favorite "first visit" questions. Since men fall in love with their eyes (the physical) and women fall in love with their ears (the character, values, the inside,) (1) what was the one unique quality that most attracted you to this person; and (2) what is the thing you would most like to change about the other?

- Cortney and Mike have given me permission to share their answers: she fell in love with his sense of humor, he fell in love with her large and trusting heart; she wants him to control his temper, he wants her not to worry so much.

- Because it was our first of 4-6 two-hour visits, they haven't decided on a theme or focus yet, but special elements are beginning to surface. Both were raised Roman Catholic and family is their number one value (they changed their wedding venue to accommodate her 80 something grandparents,) his family are half Thai and half Italian and live near the ocean. And they are adamant that their guests not bring gifts: "your presence is our present!"

- Because you never say what you don't want, but rather what you do want, I suggested that they might encourage all of their 220 guests to bring some simple symbol of love from nature—a sea shell, a flower, a twig, a rock, a leaf—and have them bring their gifts up to the bride and groom as a kind of love offering and a powerful way to get everyone involved.

  It was refreshing and reassuring to see that, as young as they are, they have a mature attitude about their wedding and their roles as hosts, and will be selfless and gracious in welcoming and involving their families and friends.

- They eagerly accepted their initial "homework" assignment: come up with a theme, begin gathering readings and musical selections around that theme, think about writing their own vows and ring blessings, and craft a love letter to each other that will provide me with an in depth personal profile of the beloved, so I can get to know each of them more deeply and intimately.

- By wedding day, the three of us will have spent a good 15 hours together—including the rehearsal and (my favorite) the rehearsal dinner where I can pick up the pulse of the families and wedding party—personalizing and spiritualizing their wedding with major emphasis on their marriage, and dozens of practical tips for handling life's and love's many challenges.

ka pule a ka haku

e ko makou makua i loko o ka lani, e hoʻanoʻia kou inoa.
our father which are in heaven, hallowed be thy name.

e hiki mai kou aupuni;
thy kingdom come

e malamaʻia kou makemake ma ka honua nei,
e like me ia i malamaʻia ma ka lani la;
thy will be done on earth, as it is in heaven

e haʻawi mai ia makou i keia la, i ʻai na makou no neia la.
give us this day our daily bread

e kala mai hoʻi ia makou i ka makou lawehala ana,
me makou e kala nei i ka poʻe i la wehala i ka makou.
and forgive us our debts, as we forgive our debtors

mai hoʻokuʻu ʻoe ia makou i ka hoʻowalewaleʻia mai;
and lead us not into temptation

e hoʻopakele no naʻe ia makou i ka ʻino;
but deliver us from evil;

no ka mea, nou ke aupuni, a me ka mana, a me ka hoʻonani ʻia, a mau loa aku.
for thine is the kingdom, and the power, and the glory, forever.

amene
amen

x

Event or Experience?

- Please begin by asking yourself: what is this all about for us as a couple? What do we want to accomplish? What is our overall purpose and intention? What do we hope to create for our families and friends?

- Over-simplified, most weddings fall into one of two broad categories: event or experience. Which do you choose?

- EVENTS are usually wonderful, lovely, very expensive parties—sometimes even spectacular parties. All the elements are professionally produced. Large, lush, grand, great! Fabulous, flamboyant happenings—fairly easily and quickly forgotten!

- EXPERIENCES are more personal, touching, and intimate celebrations—even with several hundred people—that wiggle their way into your heart and last a long time. They tend to be warm, fun, comfortable, inclusive and, best of all, involving.

- Events are out there. Experiences are in here.

- Events are produced and self-conscious. Experiences are felt and do not call attention to themselves.

Top: Jessica and Dominic continue kissing
Above: Megan and Charlie's goal was to involve everyone in their celebration

- Events invite applause. Experiences invite smiles and tears.

- Events are WOW moments. Experiences are Aha moments.

- Or, as special couple, Megan and Charlie pointed out during our salad and chardonnay marriage preparation supper recently: "Events are sex. Experiences are making love."

- We have all seen many versions of both events and experiences. If you, Dear Bride, are clear about your choice you will probably create it. If you turn it over to the bridal industry—which is of its nature impersonal and commercial—then you will get an event.

1

As Mother Theresa said so often, "It doesn't really matter what you do in this life—it's how much love you do it with!"

- The most significant ingredient in any wedding is the attitude of the bride. Will you be the hostess at a celebration of love: thanking all those people whose love for you taught you how to love?

- Do you appreciate how powerful your bridal light really is—to warm, illumine, touch, heal—everything depends on just where you point that light?

- What are the point and purpose, the meaning and message of your wedding—and this year-long incredible labor of love? Why are you doing all this?

Even if you never say a word out loud except "I do," you set the tone, project the spirit, and create the energy atmosphere for your entire wedding weekend. Does your attitude scream "It's all about me" or "Thank you for being here—you honor us with your presence?"

You are hosts rather than superstars—folks are not staring at you, you are smiling at them!

FIVE TIPS FOR A NEW BRIDE:

1. It is important that a man has a job and also helps you around the house.

2. It is important that a man makes you laugh.

3. It is important to find a man you can trust who doesn't lie to you.

4. It is important that a man loves you and spoils you.

5. It is important that these four men don't know each other.

Top: Courtney and Mark smile at their guests; Left to right: Marie Louise and Phil greet family and friends; Erin and Joe thank their guests; Libby and Ian share their happiness

He's yours! He has asked you, maybe on bended knee, to marry him, to create a covenant commitment before God and your closest family and friends, to spend the rest of your lives together, to wear his engagement ring and wedding band as everyday reminders of your unbroken and unbreakable circle of love.

You know him and love him and will pledge your life to him, in good times and bad, in health and illness, through ups and downs all the days of your lives. You also know that this wedding thing is a pretty big mystery for him. And, if you think that this is a scary challenge for him, wait until you get pregnant and prepare to bring your first child into the world.

Simply put, God has equipped you women better than men to deal with the mystery of weddings and childbirth. You have an eye—and a follow-up passion--for detail. You have an extraordinary memory. You multitask with agility and without losing focus. Your spiritual radar makes you stronger in matters of the heart.

So, please be patient with your husband-to-be. Don't expect too much. Just as you will with the miracle of birthing, invite his participation, share major decisions, and involve him as often and as intimately as he is capable.

Left: David toasts bride, Patricia; Right: Tony holds his wife, Hope

For example, your groom can and must collaborate on ring choice, wedding venue, guest list, ceremony preparation, budget, vendors and honeymoon. He will enjoy food and wine tasting, picking out gifts and favors, arranging transportation and logistics—and he may have an ear for music. But, for everyone's sake, honor his comfort zone.

Your beloved is your co-host for the entire celebration, but you enjoy experience and expertise that uniquely qualify you for things like organizing a wedding or having a baby. Your groom wants to win the Oscar for best supporting role.

Naturally, he would never buy a book like this for himself—but he may read a little over your shoulder, or peek at it when you're not around—so leave it out on the couch or coffee table.

Top: Darren snuggles new bride Alicia; Right: Joe smiles with wife Kelly

3

Your **MOTHER**

- A little history will help explain why it is that the one who "gets married" at most weddings is the mother of the bride. In brief, it is because her mother got married at her wedding and her mother got married at her wedding…and so forth.

- When I was a young priest, 45 years ago and stationed at a Mission Chapel parish that hosted as many as six to seven weddings a weekend, most brides were 18 to 23-years -old, just out of school and hadn't hosted anything as complicated as a birthday party.

- Of course, mom and dad would "throw this wedding for their little girl"—which meant, in practice, that mom would plan and dad would pay. Oh, sure, you were the recipient, the "birthday girl" so to speak, the center of attention, the bride in name—but it was basically mom's bash, her special day.

- So, please be extra patient and understanding with your parents, especially your mom. They mean well and are truly struggling to let go: of you and a family tradition (marrying off their daughter) which they controlled for generations. Listen to them and agree with almost everything as you gently nudge them from hosts to the guests of honor.

- Today's brides are mature adults, probably close to or over 30 years of age. You are professionals in the real world with your own job and your own place and eminently capable of planning and hosting your own wedding. Just remember that your mom's parents married her—they didn't only pay for it, they organized and controlled it!

- It may take time to help them realize that they have moved up from organizers and hosts to very special guests of honor, the most important people in your life, who more than anyone else on earth, loved you and taught you how to love. This is your chance to thank them, honor them and love them back. ᘓ

4

Your Mother

Photo captions from top left clockwise: Kara poses before her marriage to Adam with Mom and Dad, Joy and Vince; Janet's Mom stands on the church steps (with her yellow rose) beaming approval of her daughter's marriage to Xavier; Hope's Mom makes adjustments to her wedding dress; Erin kisses Mom and Dad a thank you; Shannon shows Mom, Liddy, her wedding dress – sadly her mother will lose her battle with cancer 5 days before the wedding

- You are preparing for a lifetime marriage, not just a weekend wedding: I often close the ceremony with a final blessing of all the couples present—as a renewal of their own love covenant—with this farewell: "Thank you for coming to the wedding; please stay for the marriage."

- Planning for the wedding is also preparation for the marriage.

- Try to meet some four to six times with your celebrant who knows a lot about weddings and even more about marriage. Most celebrants spend over half their ministry in marriage and family counseling. Take advantage of this resource and plan to meet with your celebrant several times before your wedding day.

- The Premarital Inventory, or Focus, includes 160 questions which are immensely useful tools for triggering valuable discussions about issues. For example:

  → how you would handle a child with a handicap?
  → what would you do if your spouse were unfaithful?
  → how will you deal with the in-laws?
  → what is the best way to resolve conflict?
  → which faith will we practice and raise our children in?
  → how will we handle our budget and bills, and so forth?

- Check with your church or synagogue to see what they offer in the way of prenuptial seminars and day long workshops with older couples and professional presentations. The Pre Cana Conference, or the Engaged Encounter are typical two-day weekend retreats with 20 other engaged couples and brief presentations on various potential challenges in marriage by couples who have been through it themselves—total immersion with many practical exercises (reflecting, writing, sharing) to help you prepare for your future.

Top right: Bride Shannon takes a last minute call while her sister holds the phone; Top left: Stephen, the groom, prepares; Top right: Jess and Dom prepare the seating arrangements Bottom: Jessica prepares for her wedding with Dominic

- If your own minister or church or synagogue does not offer in depth marriage preparation, can you take the initiative and go get it, because marriage, like love, is an art: first it is learned and then practiced? Please learn as much as you can before—and practice, practice, practice the rest of your life!

Sigmund Freud wrote somewhere that men and women are so different the amazing thing is that we can even talk to one another. And sometimes we can't. A husband read an article to his wife about how women average 30,000 words a day—men 15,000. The wife responded: "The reason is that we have to repeat everything to men…" The husband turned to her and asked: "What?"

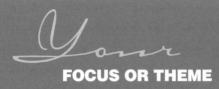

FOCUS OR THEME

"Two human loves make one divine."

Elizabeth Barrett Browning

Your Focus or Theme

6

- Have you ever noticed that most weddings have many lovely elements: cool color schemes and imaginative locations, beautiful readings, flowers, music, food and drink, wardrobe and decorations, personalized vows and love letters, a tender toast, and so forth—but don't quite gel or come together as a whole?

- How many have you attended that were great parties: wonderful food and drinks, fun music and dancing—but they didn't go anywhere, didn't touch a chord deep inside you, and didn't ever rise above the level of a "we're getting married party" which is fine if that's all you want?

- For all those individual pieces to come together and create a profound experience for your guests, you need an overall theme, a focus, a central core message, a unifying point or purpose.

- When I ask, "What is your theme?" do you know what most brides respond: "We're going with violet for the bridesmaids' dresses, white flowers on the altar, etc." and tell me what it looks like!

- It is true that men fall in love with their eyes (the outside beauty) and women fall in love with their ears (the inner values, virtues, character?) But, when it comes to weddings, the American bride is 90% visual. She is sharing her vision, her dream, and going for a look.

- Isn't equally important the content, the message, the heart of your celebration? And isn't this unifying theme one critical way to make your wedding more than an expensive party—to make it a personal experience and a sacred drama—for you and your guests?

Top left: Sherry and Doyle chose "Kukio" (Hawaiian for "rock standing strong in water") for their marriage in Hawaii Top: Janet marries chef Xavier in the wine country with a special recipe; Right: Irish Libby and Scottish Ian celebrate "unity" with their family crests; Bottom: Debra and Rich take their theme from St. Paul

- What exactly are you celebrating? Your love commitment, yes, but what is unique about your loving relationship? What is the key message and memory you want your guests to take away with them? What is this day, this event, this experience all about? Is it family, faith, fun? Is your theme trust, journey, happiness, compassion? Or perhaps gratitude, generosity, grace (always amazing) or balance? Or healing, hope, nature, God?

- What speaks to you—and of you two? Is there a picture or image or song that captures the essence of you and your wedding—remembering that the language of our age is pictures and music?

- Once you have decided on your theme or focus, begin to assemble the supporting elements that will reinforce your message—readings, symbols, actions, gifts, blessings, music, decorations, etc.—enabling you to personalize your celebration, so that when people drive or fly away after the weekend, they will say to one another: "What a powerful experience of love or joy or family! I was touched, I felt included, I felt our own love renewed."

"Love God and your neighbor and yourself—and your enemy."

Jesus of Nazareth

- Folks near death talk about two things—only and always—their family and their faith. That suggests that these two things, often taken for granted, may be the most important realities in this life.

- Your wedding is a celebration of both: Family, because two families are coming together in an intimate and inextricable bond and a whole new family (yours!) is begun; and Faith, including your awesome trust in each other, your belief in the God of love and a purpose to life, and your hope in the future.

- Involve your family as much as possible in your special day. Bridesmaids or groomsmen, greeters or ushers, as well as your parents, should provide welcome at the front door because they will recognize most of your guests. They could also offer a special toast, blessing, or prayer.

- Tell your family what you want. For example, if you want your mom to walk you down the aisle, have you asked her and let dad know what you hope he will do (sit by the aisle so you can hug him on your way in or out?). If you want both parents to escort you—most grooms and many brides today do walk in with both parents--to get away from that sexist symbol of a man giving his daughter away to another man (presumably, as in days of yore, for a dowry of three cows, two chickens and a diamond)—have you told them what you want well before, because they are subconsciously conditioned by a lifetime of Hollywood movies and mindless TV?

Top right: The Firestone family gathers after one of many weddings; Top left: The Sheridan siblings support one another; Right: Kendra and Bob blend two families; Bottom right: Libby and Ian merge families and cultures.

- Include your families in the whole enterprise by sharing: your goal, attitude, spirit, theme, hopes and dreams. Make them your biggest and best supporting cast. Make them your special guests of honor. Your loving respect for your parents and family will be felt by all— and serve as a sneak preview of how you will handle your own family someday. ⌒⌒

- What is the best number of pre-wedding parties and showers, which of course make demands on the same people—mothers, family members, and bridesmaids? Is it 4, 5, 6, at most, as most modern brides advise me?

- As fun as these parties are--and dear friends love to give them—and as useful or hysterical are the gifts—still, doesn't owning, hosting and taking charge of your wedding require boundaries and guidelines?

- What are some of the other areas where you need to establish clear limits, such as groomsmen's flasks (not for holy water,) childish pranks played with the groom's shoes ("HELP ME") or bridal rings (I think I've lost them) or rice (which is food in many cultures) or defacing your car ("Just Married") or T-P'ing your wedding suite (now we're back to high school?) What is this: a wedding or a fraternity party?

- Isn't that equally true for the traditional bachelor and bachelorette get aways? Aren't you seeking more sharing than silliness, more exercise than drinking, and more bonding than bashing?

- Don't you know that your friends love you and want to please you and are simply repeating gags they have seen at other weddings, which seemed to work? Don't most problems at weddings (and funerals) arise when your friends don't know what you want: your goals, your intention, and your spirit?

Set standards. Your family and friends want to please you; tell them how. ∽

Top left: China and America come together in Debra and Rich's wedding; Above: Dear friends give the gift of loving support.

8

- Many weddings are costly extravaganzas that have forgotten the love …and folks don't know where to go to find it…

- Money will not make or break a wedding—but a lot of love will. Whether your budget is $3,000 or $300,000, money will not have much impact on the deeper beauty and joy of your wedding.

- A fabulous wedding is full of music, spirit, and feeling. I remember over 30 years ago a simple evening wedding where the bride and groom stopped at Kentucky Fried Chicken for our reception dinner— and it was a true celebration of gracious, caring hospitality.

- Be aware, dear and vulnerable bride, that many locations and vendors, knowing that it is a wedding, actually triple their prices.

- Modern and mature brides are responsible with their budgets— whether it is their money or someone else's—and generally approximate these percentage guidelines:

A SAMPLE BUDGET: ("PIE CHART")

→ Invitations: 1%
→ Engagement/wedding rings: 5%
→ Bridal apparel: 5%
→ Wedding Program: 1%
→ Music: (wedding) 3% (reception) 4%
→ Flowers: 5%
→ Photography/videography: 10%
→ Ceremony fees: 5%
→ Attendants' gifts: 3%
→ Rehearsal dinner: 7%
→ Transportation: 1%
→ Reception: 40%
→ Honeymoon: 10%

If studies are accurate that today's weddings are averaging as much as $50,000, doesn't it seem fair to invest $20,000 in the reception and $5,000 in the honeymoon, $5,000 for photos, $3,500 for the rehearsal dinner, $3,000 for flowers, and so forth? But don't you also have your own priorities and friends and contacts and ways to save money? ∽

Top: Don't let money spoil your wedding or marriage!; Right: Bride Adrianne shows off her bargain wedding dress.

10

To be happy: free your heart from hatred, free your mind from worries, live simply, give more, and expect less. This is especially true when preparing for a wedding.

- Have you decided who will have editorial control of your guest list—and decided (usually on the basis of budget) how many and whom?

- This really is your wedding, and managing that guest list in an effective way will maintain focus and help you stay on purpose.

- Your parents are your guests of honor—and especially if they are helping pay the bills—isn't it only fair and kind to allow them to invite whomever they want? They gave you the gifts of life and love. Patiently appreciate their invitation suggestions.

- Sit down with your two families and clarify roles and responsibilities—and, most important, guest list boundaries—the more painless way to define your celebration: will you invite children, pets, dates, relatives, neighbors, work associates, golfing or bowling buddies, and so forth?

- The most competent, creative, clever brides (typically today in their late 20's or early 30's) tend to use some variation on the following approach: You ask all the most significant people in your life—including your groom and both families—to submit a wish list of their preferred guests (in order of preference.) and when there are too many on the total wish list (as always happens) then you decide on a final count and return everyone's list, asking them to cut whatever number is necessary—from the bottom up? Isn't this the most democratic American way—everyone gets a vote, everyone is included, and you are still in charge, because it's your wedding.

Top left: Kelly and Ron's families\were their guests of honor;
Above: Kelly and Joe had a large list but an imtimate wedding

A young bride-to-be learned, to her dismay, that some of her fiancé's religious beliefs were less than orthodox. "What shall I do?" she asked her mother anxiously, "Harold doesn't even believe in hell." "Don't worry, dear," her mother replied, "between the two of us, we'll show him how wrong he is."

Y INVITATION

"Carpe Diem—seize the day!"

This is an opportunity to create your first impression, a chance to set the tone and spirit of your wedding. You can use variations on a personalized message. I received this recently in the mail: "Because you have shared in our lives by your friendship and love…" all on a single small sheet of opaque stationery tied with white ribbon to an artistically designed and colorful blotter background. Unique and lovely—and clearly a labor of love that took thought and effort.

- Smart brides have even designed an invitation/response card, where the response card is attached by perforation to the bottom third of the invitation to be returned postcard style—less paper and less postage.

  Add a personal touch with the new personalized postage stamps you can order from the post office—with your names right on the stamp itself.

- Bride Melissa hand made each of her 120 invitations with artistic, tender, loving care, so that they served as love letters and a sneak preview of the wedding everyone now looked forward to attending. Little things mean a lot—especially in matters of the heart.

- Thermography costs much less than expensive engraving and is equally attractive for your printed invitations. Also, shop those post-holiday sales by stationers and printing companies. Or consider buying all your paper goods (save-the-date cards, invitations, programs, menus, thank you cards, and so on) from the same place —to save both time and treasure—while you create your own look.

*Top: Katie and Brian, their dog and the lake;
Right: Jacque and Teddy mug for love.*

- Incidentally, those increasingly popular "Save-The-Date" cards are a wonderful opportunity to personalize and add a dash of flair to your wedding experience. Jacque and Teddy and Leslie and Nick had great fun making theirs—with little more than a photo booth and Kinko's. Rebecca and Mark's card, like many, had a magnet so it stuck to the fridge. Jess and Dom featured their beloved flower hound on the cover. Brenda and Gordie sent out Save the Weekend cards with a sketch of two very hot tamales to announce their wedding in Cabo San Lucas, Mexico. And one of the most creative Save the Date cards I've ever received came attached to a lovely silver cork screw announcing Amanda and Tyler's wedding in the Napa wine country.

- Click on some of these helpful sites: www.rexcraft.com (mail order invitations) or www.crane.com (for a free glance at their 159 page wedding etiquette blue book for etiquette obsessed brides) or www. paper-source.com (to create original stationery, cards, invitations and programs) or www.invitesite.com (kits for creating your own with pressed flowers and handmade paper)

Your location, location, location...

- Your wedding weekend is like a wedding ring, and your ceremony or service is the diamond sparkling in the center. Choose your location first and then build everything else around and near it.

- What is the number one quality you look for in a wedding venue:beauty, service, low cost—or convenience? Make sure your wedding venue reflects you and not a Hollywood movie. What really matters and makes sense—to you and your guests? What spaces best support your celebration?

- Distance: How far is your reception from your wedding? For your guests' sake, have you considered practicalities like driving, parking, comfort—because nothing kills the mood and magic of a great wedding like a half hour drive?

- Weather: What kind of weather can you expect on your wedding weekend? Do you have back-up plans?

- Options: Have you checked out:

  → All inclusive venues that specialize in weddings and offer package deals including flowers, food, decorations and cake?

  → Banquet halls and hotels (that might charge for the use of their space) or bed and breakfast inns, historic buildings, parks and wineries that sometimes stock wedding supplies like tables, chairs, linen, and tableware?

  → If you are being wed in a house of worship, do they have a hall you might rent, fix up and promise to clean up?

Top left: Cortney and Mike stroll along a nearby beach after their wedding
Left above: Jenny and Michael picked the country church from Hitchcock's "The Birds";
Top: Ranny and Bob in Positano; Bottom: Leslie and Nick celebrated in a Seattle cathedral

- Sites: Check into some creative sites for ideas on wedding venues like www.weekendwinery.com (national winery guide) or www.towd.com (worldwide directory of tourist offices) or www.nps.gov (national parks site) or www.thebarnjournal.org (beautiful barns for rent) or www. museumlink.com/states.htm (museum web sites nationwide?)

- Appreciation: Most important, are your wedding venues conducive to the spirit, atmosphere and feeling you want everyone to experience? Is your rehearsal dinner site well suited for toasting and roasting (which is why we come—and not to eat?) Does your reception location allow you and your new husband to move easily among your guests sharing your happiness, affection and gratitude for the gift of their presence (which is why you invited them—and not for presents and applause?)

As Billy Crystal has observed: "Women need a reason to have sex. Men just need a place."

- May I call this person "celebrant" rather than "officiant"—hoping you will want a celebration more than an official service?

- Do you know and like him or her? Prayerful spirituality? Common sense intelligence? Calming sense of humor?

- Will your minister, rabbi, priest, judge or justice of the peace take the time to really get to know you (at least 6-8 hours over 3-4 appointments)?

- Is she or he willing to personalize your celebration—flexible, accommodating, and experienced—or will it be another out-of-the-book ritual as usual?

- Does your celebrant help you prepare for a lifetime marriage as well as a weekend wedding?

- What pre-nuptial resources—readings, questionnaires, seminars, retreats—are offered?

- Will your wedding minister (I think of them as masters of ceremonies) also lead the rehearsal, which is less about processing and blocking and more about aligning your core group—families and wedding party—in that spirit you desire for the wedding?

- What is his or her level of participation and will they attend your rehearsal dinner and reception and be available for a blessing or two?

- What are the usual fees--$500 to $5000 (you usually get what you pay for)—and what services (preparation and participation) are included?

Left: Catholic Carol marries Jewish Steven;
Right: Marie Louise and Phil and Celebrant are all smiling.

- Different faith traditions: Roman Catholics are very serious about marriage (and wedding) preparation: 6-12 months, premarital counseling (Pre-Cana) baptismal certificates, freedom to marry signed by witnesses, and certificates of annulment if you were married before. Protestant ministers differ greatly but most also require some months of serious preparation with the minister or at a parish program. Jews often have the most and best marital traditions and ceremonies—and charge the highest fees. Couples meet with their rabbi beforehand and the bride may be required to visit the mikvah bath for a ritual cleansing. Sometimes the groom on the Sabbath before the wedding has an aufruf at which he is called to read from the Torah and afterwards candy and sweets are thrown at him as wishes for a sweet life.

- Have you checked websites like www.weddingministers.com (with 3000 ministers, priests, rabbis and justices in the U.S.—plus ideas for your vows and readings)? And, better yet, have you "shopped around" a bit and seen some celebrants in action? Your wedding is too important to rely on a web site or whoever's on duty at the local church or temple.

Your Celebration

14

Your Wardrobe

- Your wardrobe is another area where more is not necessarily better—and where less (money and frills) is often more.

- Is your bridal gown just a Cinderella shopping trip—or does it make a statement about you?

- Does your wedding dress really work for a hostess bride—with immense leadership responsibilities at the ceremony, the meal and on the dance floor? Or are you thinking mostly photo op?

- Do your light and beauty shine from within—like stained glass windows—or is your light really a spotlight and your beauty store bought?

- If smart brides shop at full service bridal stores that offer a wide variety and are able to provide alterations, then don't really smart and budget conscious brides check out pre-owned or demo gowns and get them tailored and enhanced?

- One bride, realizing that neither she nor her bridesmaids would ever wear their dresses again, told her attendants to choose whatever dress they wanted in sage green, as long as they would indeed wear it again! Make all payments—including down payments—with a credit card for your own protection.

- Can't your groom explore formal wear shops that offer packaged deals—e.g. his is free if all the groomsmen rent their tuxedos there as well—or couldn't he consider investing in his first tux, if he will wear it 2-3 times a year?

Top left: Jenny and Michael go multicultural! Above left: a gown hangs ready; Top right: Kendi and Bob focused on the inside, the heart, the love; Bottom: Cortney "Leis" Michael in the Hawaiian tradition.

- Have you looked into these web sites for good deals on accessories: www.bluefly.com (discount designer site—75% off retail on everything from shoes to earrings) www.veilshop.com (tutorial on different lengths and styles of veils and how to avoid wrinkles) www.myglassslipper.com (everything you wanted to know about bridal footwear) www.makeup411.com (inside secrets from makeup pros) and, of course, www.ebay.com/wedding (auction site for all your wedding day stash?)

When the late Mr. and Mrs. Henry Ford celebrated their Golden Wedding Anniversary, a reporter asked them: "To what do you attribute your 50 years of successful married life?" "The formula," said Ford, "is the same formula I have always used in making cars—just stick to one model!"

- Wedding rings are the most wonderful symbols: of beauty, treasure and your unbroken covenant of love—no beginning, no end, a powerful, non-verbal reminder of your eternal circle of love! (P.S. Get the comfort fit, non-pinch curved interior and have them engraved.)

- You know how to find your rings: check with others, shop together, go online for wholesale jewelers or diamond dealers—and isn't the most precious and personal (and economical) tradition to "recycle" jewels that have been in the family for years like a diamond from grandma's ring? If you two have not picked out your rings yet, you might take the Gemological Institute of America's free tutorial: it's the best primer on the four C's of diamond value.

- Rings can run from $50 to $50,000! Least expensive is the 14-karat gold band, 18-karat gold is next, and platinum is the most expensive—although white gold can provide the same look for less.

- Why not write your own blessing prayer—perhaps even including a short description of your rings and the story behind them? What will you have inscribed inside your wedding band: "forever" "semper amemus" (Latin for "Let us love always") "eternal love" or your favorite blessing? Is there a story behind your rings and, most importantly, what do they mean to you? (Why should this be a private little secret rite between you and your minister?) The traditional blessings are: "With this ring, I thee wed…" or "Take and wear this ring as a sign of our marriage vows…" easily personalized and improved on!

- And why not share the blessing of the rings with your families and attendants (who usually have little else to do but sit and count the minutes until the chilled champagne?) Couldn't your minister or priest bring the rings—once God has blessed them—to the wedding party and immediate family so that each of them might press a silent prayer or blessing into these symbols you will wear for the rest of your lives? Let your Celebrant know how you want to personalize this meaningful ring exchange.

- And, if you have the time and courage, wouldn't the most dramatic and moving ceremony be you and your new husband, with ringed hands joined, moving around the Assembly so that they are blessing not just the rings but your hands—and you?

Prior to the 5th century, the ring finger was the index finger. Later it was believed that the third finger contained the "vein of love" that led directly to the heart.

16

Your Vendors

- Do you know who the potential enemies of a great wedding are? Would you believe, in most cases, they are your hired hands, the people you are paying to work for you, your vendors?

- Aren't some mess-ups and mistakes understandable and excusable: like your baker goofs on the cake, your florist mismatches flowers and color schemes, your beauticians run late, your sound man blows a fuse, your caterer can't keep the food hot, your officiant is grouchy and impersonal, your candles blow out? Aren't these slips human and forgivable?

- But what about the DJ who turns your reception into a teen dance, or the wedding assistant who thinks it's HER day and bosses everyone around, causing uncomfortable delays, or your #1 enemy with the most powerful weapon (a camera), your photographer, who knows that more photos usually means more profit.

The vendors you choose are critical to the success of your wedding celebration!

- And don't they all say the "right thing" or just what you want to hear—and then do their controlling or commercializing thing at your wedding when you are powerless to manage them and have far more important responsibilities than overseeing the hired help?

- How can you protect yourself? Always check references, get agreements in writing, pay with credit cards (keeps a record, protects your deposits and can help settle disputes) and watch out for "hidden costs" like sales tax, gratuities, overtime, extra staff, special equipment, etc.?

In the Art of Loving, Erich Fromm sums up: "Love is the only sane and satisfactory answer to the problem of human existence."

- Isn't music the language of love? Isn't music—along with pictures—the language of our age? Aren't words, however beautiful, even classical, always limited when it comes to expressing our deepest human emotions and the mystery of love? Why do you suppose the film industry puts so much into musical backgrounds and movie sound tracks? Isn't music more important than flowers or food or photographs? And does your budget reflect that priority?

- Music touches the soul, conveys the ineffable, and creates a mood, spirit, and feeling. For a big band sound minus the expense hire a small ensemble of four musicians with a keyboardist who can use a synthesizer to preprogram string, horn and percussion sections. Do you have a talented friend who can play a musical meditation between your readings or after your vows. The half hour of calming music BEFORE the service is vitally important as it sets a tone and relaxes everyone.

- Doesn't music wiggle into our subconscious and linger longer? Isn't this exactly your priority and where you want to make your unique, personal statement and put your finger print or heart print? And isn't it like everything else in your celebration: the more personal, the more powerful—and memorable?

- If you and your groom have "tin ears," get a friend who is musically savvy to advise and guide you. Of course, it is always better if the musical menu—for the whole wedding weekend—comes from your favorites, your memories, and your heart.

- Visit these internet sites: www. soi.org Symphony Orchestra Institute which links to 140 symphonic groups in the U.S. with professional musicians who moonlight at weddings; www.wedalert.com/songs features 1200 snippets of music for ceremony, first dance, ethnic input; www.adaj.org the American Disc Jockey Association with hiring tips (equipment, insurance, contracts) and average rates; www.booklivemusic.com offers musical samples of hundreds of bands and classical musicians nationwide. And, last but not least, www.bustamove.com provides easy-to-follow instructions and pictures to help you and your beloved brush up on your Fred Astaire and Ginger Rogers dance floor excellence.

Top left: Trios work well in church and at the reception; Top right: Some tunes need acoustical guitarists like Rob; Bottom: for processions bag pipers and drums work well.

Top right: Many local boys and girls church and school choirs love to sing at weddings; Bottom left: Jennifer and Michael's India/American wedding with sitar

Your CATERER

- What is it about food service and caterers that makes them such generally supportive contributors to your celebration? Is it the profound spirituality of food—sharing, nourishing, energizing—an incredible intimacy: we make it one with us, a true holy communion? You don't have to be Jewish or Italian to appreciate that sharing food is a powerful way to say, "I love you!"

- Because fantasy and excitement drive the bridal biz, have you thoroughly checked out such a big ticket item as your caterer: at least three personal recommendations from friends, at least three professional references from satisfied brides, and your own local Better Business Bureau for any history of complaints?

- Have you reviewed and signed a written contract, had a trusted friend double-check it for you, and agreed to always pay by credit card (never cash or check) in order to keep a valid record and enable your credit card company to investigate and resolve any disputes?

Top left and right: Food says "I love you"; Bottom left: Sydney planned a white wedding cake and a chocolate piano grooms cake for Scott.

- Have you done your internet homework; www.icacater.org refers you to the International Catering Association and the best chefs in America; www.rentalhq.com for your local party rental stores plus many professional tips on the practicalities; www.wineanswers.com for detailed help on the number of bottles to buy, correct serving temperatures, or how to chill a chardonnay in 30 minutes; I'll skip the sites for hard alcohol which tends to hurt more than help at weddings—and, of course, you'll have an open bar—or no bar at all; www.chefmike.com by Chef Mike Collins, author of "Cater Your Own Wedding" offers suggestions for everything from how much ice to buy to the question of including children in your head count.

Top: Sweets for the sweet; Bottom left: Patrice and Michael's fabulous reception dinner; Bottom right: a caterer adds a creative touch.

18

Your Caterer

- Most so-called wedding coordinators tend to be "party planners" with controlling attitudes and rigid rules and a concept of weddings somewhere between a Junior Prom and the runway at a fashion show. Many churches have hired and trained their own coordinators who have some sense of the sacred and understand that your wedding is not the Miss America Beauty Pageant.

- Of course, they are well intentioned and have every moment of your wedding on their laptop—names, numbers, logistics, minutiae—unfortunately without any sense of the spiritual or appreciation of the deeper meaning of the moment, the drama, the celebration that transcends pomp and circumstance. They tend to organize events—they do not create shared experiences.

- Yes, they take charge of the details—do they ever—so you don't have to worry about them—but I fear their concept of weddings is derived from Hollywood and TV wedding imitations. Please forgive my candor, dear bride, but these coordinators you hire (get it: they work for you!) to help execute the little things will always say the "right thing" or exactly what you want to hear but they must be given clear and explicit guidance from you: be firm and make it clear who is in charge—especially of the big picture.

- For example, watch out for their sense of timing. Because they tend to take charge of everything, personally cueing decorations, music, bridal party, food service, etc., your wedding schedule can be off by 15 to 60 minutes. When you announce in a printed invitation that your wedding will begin at 5 p.m., it is rude, unkind, and foolish to keep 150 people waiting for the 10-15 who always arrive late—even sillier to keep everyone waiting for your coordinator's starting flag.

- Naturally, emergencies arise—and sometimes you need to adjust and accommodate—but your hired help should not be part of the problem. And, as you might imagine, once your wedding weekend has arrived, it's too late to coach the person who was supposed to be your administrative assistant. My experience with coordinators suggests that they learned their trade planning parties and handling conferences. Your wedding is far more sacred category!

- In sum, if you need an administrative aide or assistant producer, check several references, interview thoroughly and, as with any serious contract, be crystal clear about what you want—and don't want. Some can actually save you money through their professional contacts. Some charge a flat fee—some charge 15-20% of the total cost of your wedding—some charge by the hour. Some bridal consultants will come in just for the day to manage the festivities. Whatever you decide, make it clear that it's your wedding—in every way, at every moment—not theirs.

- You can check referrals through the Association of Bridal Consultants (860-355-0464) or the Association of Certified Wedding Consultants (860-520-2292) or the Association for Wedding Professionals International (800-242-4461) or on the net www.junewedding.com. As always, the best referrals come from trusted friends who found a winner.

PHOTOGRAPHER

Love Story suggested that "love means never having to say you're sorry." In fact, love means being able to say you're sorry!

- Dear Bride, I hope you will forgive me for pointing out that your photographer can be (unwittingly) the number one enemy of a great wedding—AND is armed with the most powerful weapon at your wedding. They can point that camera at anyone—individual or group, blushing bride or intoxicated usher—and make them do whatever they want.

- In 45 years, I have worked with many hundreds of honorable and talented photographers—but, on the battlefield of your wedding, something happens. I have seen photographers keep people in the church for over an hour after a 45- minute ceremony—IN ORDER TO TAKE AND SELL MORE PICTURES.

- I have even witnessed weddings where the photographer dares to take the bride and groom away from their own wedding to some artsy photo op location that had nothing to do with the wedding except that it was pretty and reasonably nearby. What's wrong with this picture?!

Yes, of course, they will always say the right and practical thing—and exactly what you want to hear: "I will be invisible and in the background, capturing the moment, the spontaneous, the authentic," and so forth… Guess what, they know that their best shots are the "set ups"—well lit, blocked, staged—and that's where the money is!. You probably won't believe this but many brides have told me that their best and most precious wedding photos were taken not by a pro but by a dear and loving friend who just loves to take pictures—for free.

- What to do to restore focus? First of all, do the research: check with trusted friends, get personal references for at least three professionals, check out samples of their work, and then make your choice on the basis of chemistry, intuition and your sixth sense.

- Reject any "coverage package" or "album presale" and negotiate with your chosen photographer to own your negatives (you will save a bundle on the cost of making prints for yourself, your family and friends!) and explain kindly but firmly that you will appoint one of your close friends as "photo producer." Preferably someone who knows most of the members of your two families, your "Photo Producer" or "picture coordinator" will have from you a clipboard with a list of all the shots—set ups and candids (in general)—that you will want to capture for sure. This person will represent you and work with your photographers who in turn will take direction from your producer. You simply will not—and cannot—be bothered by such details during your celebration—anymore than you would want to oversee the caterers in the kitchen!

- Incidentally, this is not a "job" for your (or the hotel's or resort's or club's) wedding coordinator who doesn't really know any of your family or guests. You want a take-charge but friendly face with a list of the 15-20 pictures you want to be sure to capture, with appropriate time lines—someone who will really enjoy taking this photo-coordinating responsibility off your shoulders and off your mind.

- Once those 20 or so key shots are covered, the photographer can roam creatively and take those random shots—folks in transition, at table, on the dance floor, and so forth—that capture the feel and spirit of a wedding—the kind of imaginative insights that great photographers are able to find and capture on film.

Top: You want to find a photographer,
like Kris, who can capture the "shots" between the "shots"!

- Helpful websites include: www.weva.com "Find a Videographer" lists professionals in your area, tips on best coverage, and the latest trends in video styles. www.ofoto.com enables you to create an on-line photo album which family and friends can view for free—uploading and editing and ordering prints is simple. www.ppa.com allows you to search the Professional Photographers of America member database by city or zip code—with tips on how to interview your prospective photographer.

Chosing the right photographer is essential!

- Flowers are like music—they go where mere words cannot—they tickle the memory, nudge the imagination, awake the senses, and touch the soul.

- The biggest flower buying day of your life will probably be your wedding. Mother's Day, Valentine's Day, Easter Sunday are all runners up. Bridal bouquet, attendants' bouquets, boutonnieres for your groom, groomsmen, and fathers, corsages for your mothers, flowers to decorate church and centerpieces for your reception tables and maybe even more for your flower girl, decorating your cake and dressing up those buffet tables!

- Choose flowers that are in season at the time of the wedding
    - → hand-tied stems over elaborate bouquets
    - → loose cut flowers in vases over sculpted centerpieces
    - → go to www.ccfc.org or just ask your florist to help you determine what is in season

- Ask if other weddings are scheduled for your church or synagogue or venue the same weekend. Offer to coordinate floral arrangements with the other brides and split the cost two or three ways.

- Hold your wedding near a holiday—Christmas, Easter, Thanksgiving, even Fourth of July—when these places will already be festively appointed with greenery, lights, bows, banners and lovely floral arrangements.

- Consider God's outdoor cathedrals or Mother Nature's sanctuaries for your venue: parks, beaches, botanical gardens, country clubs.

- Personalize your celebration: bring your own vases, maybe even use Grandma's silver.

Top left and right: The beauty and majesty of mother nature; Bottom left: Kristi and Drew's flowered logo.

- Ask for a dry-run bouquet for your formal portrait (which should be done several weeks before the wedding)

- Check out florist accreditation
    - → American Institute of Floral Designers at www.aifd.org
    - → Society of American Florists at www.saf.org

- IMPORTANCE: Imagine the ceremony itself as the diamond and everything else—before and after—the wedding band. Isn't this what it's really all about? Invest as much time, thought and money in the service as the other elements and moments, important as they are.

- ENTRANCE: The most beautiful, powerful, unforgettable weddings I have experienced began with the bride and groom together welcoming their guests as they arrived. (Still, I know that the pompous procession will take several generations to evolve.) The best, most meaningful giving of bride and groom to one another always involved both sets of parents (even if remarried.) We haven't asked "Who gives this woman…" or "If anyone knows any reason why she should not marry…" for almost 40 years—although a neat switch is to ask the whole congregation for their affirmation of this union, so that in a sense everyone present "gives" them to one another.

- WELCOME: Whether you have one long, lovely procession or 4-6 shorter, separate processions (like the movies and your best friend's wedding,) eventually all are in place and someone needs to greet the assembly with tender loving care. It can be your minister but is a lot warmer if one or both of you turn to your family and friends at the very beginning and offer a very brief greeting and thank you. (See: Chapter 25, Your Rehearsal.)

- OPENING PRAYER: You can compose a brief formal prayer that sets the spiritual, transcendent tone of your wedding or your celebrant can create one in keeping with your overall theme…As a last resort, you can choose one from a prayer book or wedding ritual. (For ideas, check out Chapter 33.) And, remember, one of your most important prayers is the so-called Prayer of the Faithful—in which you propose special intentions and ask your guests to respond prayerfully—especially significant are your remembrances, by name, of those who have died or are with you in spirit!

- READINGS: The key here is to choose selections that reinforce your theme so that the ceremony builds in meaning—perhaps two readings from sacred scripture and two from poetry or other moving excerpts—and find great readers to bring them alive! (Refer to Chapter 35.)

- REFLECTIONS OR SERMON: This is why it is so critical that your officiant get to know you both well, so she or he can tie all the prayers and readings together—not just to your theme or ceremony focus but to you and your loved ones. This is also why I recommend that you "arm" your celebrant with "Love Letters" to help give an x-ray profile of the two of you and your unique love. (See the examples on page 40.)

- VOWS: Traditional vows are fine—you might substitute "all the days of our lives" for "until death do us part"—but here's another opportunity to put your fingerprint or heart print on your wedding and make it yours and not just another tired cookie-cutter, out-of-the-book look and sound alike. Vows basically make three promises: I give me to you, I accept the gift of you to me, and it's forever. You don't have to memorize them and read off an index card in your hand. Let your celebrant read your vows to you (quietly) phrase by phrase so you can proclaim them loudly and proudly to all. (Check examples on page 43.)

Left: Leslie and Paolo light their Unity Candle; Right: Tony waits for Hope —with hope!

24

Your Ceremony

- RINGS: After asking God's blessing on these powerful symbols of unbroken, eternal love, I usually take the rings to the wedding party (who have almost nothing else to do, anyway) and ask them to press their own silent blessing into the rings and then do the same with the immediate family—they are honored and deeply grateful to be an integral part of this ring blessing. Then the bride and groom exchange their rings with one another. (If time and your comfort level allow, consider joining your ringed hands and asking all your guests for their blessing—incredibly intimate and moving!)

- SYMBOLS OF UNITY: Most brides are familiar with the Unity Candle rite: your parents come up and light the side tapers, passing the light and love of the family on to their daughter and son (don't do this before the ceremony—it's a beautiful essential part) and then the bride and groom take their individual candles and light the larger single candle in the middle, two become one. I used to suggest that they then blow out their own candles—until during a rehearsal about 35 years ago, a bride said "No way, padre, I'm not blowing me out—I'm still me!" I agreed and thanked her for her insight: good psychology and good theology. You create a new oneness in your marriage covenant—but you're still you, two separate people: with God's grace, one plus one equals three.

(Other symbols of your oneness are mentioned on page 44, Your Symbols of Unity.)

Jane and Tom exchange their vows before her Rabbi and his Priest in their backyard tent-temple.

- GUEST PARTICIPATION: One of the absolute keys to an extra-ordinary wedding is making your guests not spectators but participants. Catholics have a relatively effortless way to do this by involving their guests in the celebration of Mass: with well known prayers, rituals, often music, Holy Communion, and so on. But there are many other ways to actively include your family and friends in your wedding—at the very least with a familiar prayer like the Lord's Prayer and a greeting of peace where all your guests simply turn to one another and exchange a handshake or hug and the blessing: "God's peace be with you!" Many brides will arrange to have a couple of long stemmed roses hidden near the front, which the couple can take to their mothers as a surprise, perhaps during the peace greeting. More ambitious and imaginative brides may include a gift offering where each person brings to the bride and groom some symbol of love (flower, rock, twig, sea shell…) something for the couple to keep as a memento of this celebration.

• CONCLUSION: Such spiritual interaction—whether a peace offering, a communion service, presentation of a symbolic gift, or simply communal prayer—brings your sacred drama from its climax (exchange of vows and rings at which time you marry each other) to its conclusion. Most religious denominations close with a special blessing—often called the nuptial blessing—for the newest couple among us. Another lovely, thoughtful way to include your guests as participants is to share that blessing with all present, especially couples, and invite them to use this blessing as a renewal of their own love commitment. I usually ask everyone to stand and take the hand of their loved one and make the intention to renew their own covenant. It may be, for them, the most important moment at your wedding and, in any case, they will thank you for your sensitive thoughtfulness!

All of that corny pomposity about "I now pronounce you man (person) and wife (relationship)" and "You may kiss the bride" (another sexist hangover) has pretty much faded away, thank God, but your celebrant might conclude by suggesting that we seal the sacred promise and ceremony with a kiss. In Roman times a kiss was seen as a legal bond that sealed all contracts, and has become a staple ending to a wedding ceremony. People love that final kiss and immediately break into applause and you turn and exit slowly, thanking all and loving all with your eyes and smile. And, naturally, you begin by going together as a married couple for the first time to your parents and family—making it clear to all who your guests of honor were. ◯

Top: Megan and Dan do what many couples do not: enjoy their own wedding!;
Bottom: Leslie and Paolo symbolize "Two-Becoming-One"

REHEARSAL

Your Rehearsal

"Make me an instrument of your peace. Where there is hatred, let me sow love. Where there is doubt, faith. Where there is despair, hope. Where there is darkness, light. Where there is sadness, joy. Grant that I may not so much seek to be consoled as to console, to be understood as to understand, to be loved as to love. For it is in giving that we receive. It is in pardoning that we are pardoned. It is in dying that we are born to eternal life."

St. Francis of Assisi

- Good weddings take 45 minutes (which is the American attention span—60 minutes and you've lost them; 20 minutes and people wonder: "I shaved my legs for this?")—good rehearsals take 90 minutes, if they really do their job!

- It took me about six years and 300 weddings to figure out that rehearsals are not about blocking (the logistics drill: order and positions)—which could have been handled much more efficiently by fax or e-mail! The whole point of a rehearsal is the bonding of your two families and wedding party and, most importantly, the creation of a common spirit, attitude, and focus (back to your overall theme—what is this celebration all about?!) 10% of any group can control the feel, spirit, and dynamic of the whole group! So, if you plan to host 250 guests at your wedding, you need only 25 people at your rehearsal to become of one mind and attitude so they can help you host this celebration of love.

- I love these "teachable moments"—in fact, I may be one of the only priests or wedding celebrants left in America who still leads the rehearsal and it distresses me that most wedding venues have "hired" the rehearsal out for $50 or so, because the celebrant can't stand the tension. It's not just a chalk-talk-walk-through, but a spiritual attitude adjustment. I consider your rehearsal an integral part of your whole wedding experience.

Some critical points to cover at your rehearsal:

- Rehearsals and weddings now start at the appointed time—late is no longer "fashionable" but rude and unkind and makes you look scattered, ditsy and self-absorbed.

- Rehearsals begin with a greeting from the bride and groom who then turn it over to the celebrant for an opening prayer to ask God's blessing on everyone and every element of the celebration.

Top left: Kristi and Drew;
Left: Jennifer and Michael;
Right: Francie and Patrick

- Greeters and Ministers of Hospitality: Both families have this most important role. Every person who comes to your wedding should be greeted by name and welcomed at the front door.

- Ushers need a bit of coaching: "ushing" is an extension of hospitality. The usher extends his hands, shares his name, thanks them for coming, and walks with them to an open seat (picking sides is unnecessary). Late arrivals will find their way to an open seat.

- Line up: It is usually easiest to have everyone line up in front, near the altar or sanctuary, where they will end up at the conclusion of the procession (The order or formation—by size or by couples or however you envision your wedding party assembled—for the ceremony should ideally have been worked out by you well ahead of time and emailed or faxed to everyone so they know their place) The bride and groom are front and center, whatever the venue, facing one another and turned slightly toward their families and guests—with your wedding party gathered around you in supportive fashion, facing the couple, not the congregation—this is not the photo op; the minister faces the assembly when speaking to them directly and faces the couple when addressing them (with his back to the people)—no one goes to a wedding to see the celebrant!

Top: Sienna and Peter; Left: Patrice and Michael; Right: Megan and Charlie

- Procession: This procession at the official start of your formal celebration is so important that it deserves its own chapter ("Your Procession.") The key thing to rehearse is the attitude or spirit of your support team—official witnesses—as they enter: are they smiling and greeting guests with their eyes ("Thank you for coming—you honor us with your presence!") or are they nervously, self consciously thinking: "I'm so excited, …" It relaxes everyone if they all enter in pairs, escorted, in keeping with the spirit of married coupling, and warmly (non-verbally) welcome your guests, as they would if this were your home.

- Nerves: A few of my grooms have passed out during the wedding—and lots of bridesmaids and groomsmen—but never a bride. Still, it is always a good idea to remind folks to stand with knees slightly bent, bridesmaids holding bouquets usually and groomsmen with their hands at their sides. ∽

29

30

- VIDEO/AUDIO TAPE IT: You will probably look back on this evening as one of the most tender, intimate, joyful, loving, fun experiences of your life, and certainly your whole wedding weekend. (It has always been my favorite part of the wedding experience.) So get a friend to videotape it or at least audio record this precious, once-in-a-lifetime celebration, so you can play it back on anniversaries, or when you're feeling a bit sad or underappreciated. Every couple wishes they had and almost everyone forgets.

- NOT A MEAL, BUT A LOVE FEAST: While it is called a "dinner" and does involve eating, it is not primarily a meal. Rather it is a glorious public storytelling love feast! The dinner is only the context, the setting, the environment—not the primary purpose. We are not there to eat—but to toast and thank, to remember and dream.

- WHAT MATTERS: Because this is first a sharing and only secondly a meal, the important part is not the menu, food service or wine list. The main question to be asked when selecting a site for your rehearsal dinner is: where can we comfortably and conveniently gather with family and friends for a quiet celebration before the formal celebration of our wedding?

- LOGISTICS: Can everyone see and hear one another clearly and easily? Is there a platform or podium? Will a microphone be available? Will all your guests be comfortable for several hours? Are you assured of no noisy distractions from other diners?

- GEOGRAPHY: Is your dinner site close enough to your rehearsal site that folks don't have to drive many miles for many minutes? Try to find a place within five miles and 10-15 minutes at most.

- HOTEL VS. RESTAURANT VS. CLUB: Remember, you are not looking for a great restaurant, but a great place to share stories, giggles, tears and love. Homes work wonderfully for pre-wedding parties, and also for rehearsal dinners in one large room or patio where everyone can fit comfortably

- M. C.: The evening needs a master of ceremonies—often the father or mother of the groom if they are paying for everything. Sometimes the bride and the groom, as the hosts for the whole wedding weekend, will welcome everyone as they sit down, thank their parents or relatives or friends who made the evening possible, ask their minister for a blessing and then begin the dinner proper by introducing members of their wedding party –with a creative thank you gift for each. That way we all know who they are and how they are connected to the bride and groom when they stand up later to share a love story or a fond memory. Remember to give each other a little love gift as well.

- BEGIN EARLY WITH TOASTs: Do not make the mistake of waiting until everyone has finished their main course, or some other Emily Post protocol, as if this were a dinner party. Start the toasts early; that's why we are here. You have already set the tone for the evening with your introductions and gifts. Now is the time to give those who love you most a chance to express their happiness and affection for you.

- STARTERS: It usually helps to have several key people primed ahead of time, so they can begin the toasts. Never allow anyone to "save" their toast or speech for your reception. In fact, you can tell your maid of honor and your best man that they will enjoy ten times the attention at the rehearsal dinner which is an intimate setting for tender talks. They might save one fun, delightful personal story to share at the reception.

- Wise Timing: Wrap up the evening at a decent hour, before 10 p.m., so everyone can enjoy a little beauty rest and prepare for the celebration of your wedding. Wisely discourage late night drinking and partying—especially for your families and wedding party—you will need their bright eyed presence and alert help for the main event.

- FIRST IMPRESSION: You might think what does it matter how we all arrive? Who cares? True, it's not the most important part of your ceremony—but it is the first impression and your opportunity to set a tone, create a feeling, and make a personal statement.

- PERSONALIZE: This is really the beginning of your wedding. Why not lighten up, have some fun, and make it reflect your values, your personality, and your marriage?

- EVERYONE IS ESCORTED: Have you watched a loving couple walking together? Almost always hand in hand or arm in arm! Isn't that the image, symbol, spirit you want for your wedding? Don't you really want everyone to enter escorted, to process in as couples? Why do some weddings work so hard to make sure every guest is escorted by an usher or groomsman—and certainly every parent and grandparent—and then separate the men and women in your wedding party and allow the bridesmaids to make their own way down the aisle?

Left: Phil is escorted bvy Mom and Dad; Right: A beautiful garden procession.

In 45 years and 2000 weddings, I've seen everything.

- WORST CASE SCENARIO: separate processions (with separate songs) for grandparents (ageist,) mothers (sexist,) bridesmaids (separatist,) and, finally, bride and father (presumably a hangover from the dowry days when dad would "sell" his little girl to the groom for 3 cows, 2 chickens and a goat (more if she had a college education and dental work!)

- BEST CASE SCENARIO: after welcoming all their guests at the front door of the church or wedding venue (the way you would welcome guests to your own home) the entire family, in fact both families enter in one long reverent procession (with bright cheerful musical accompaniment) often led by sets of grandparents, celebrant, the groom with mom and dad on either side, the bridesmaids and groomsmen, two by two (including whatever children and pets should be included) and, finally, at the conclusion of the bridal procession (singular!) accompanied by the mother and father who brought her into the world and accompanied her through life so far, the bride.

Top: Harry is escorted by Mom, Roseline, and Dad, Harry;
Bottom: Alicia is escorted by Mom,
Sandy and Dad, Bernie

Top: Ranny and Bob welcome their guests to their wedding celebration in Postitano, Italy Above: Megan is led into her reception by Charlie on a donkey who thought all the applause was for him

- ATTITUDE: All these folks enter smiling, greeting the guests with unselfconscious eyes that say "Thank you for coming!"—especially the groom and his parents and the bride and her parents. This mind set or attitude must be practiced at the rehearsal, because most people find entrance processions extremely uncomfortable, nerve wracking challenges. In fact, focusing on your guests and the assembly takes the pressure off you and puts the emphasis on welcoming your guests.You already possess the light—inside and out—shine it on those you love!

- OPTIONS: Although in our country most wedding parties seem to end up on the altar or in front of their families and friends as if lining up for a photo op, many today gather in a warm supportive semicircle around the bride and groom—sometimes with women and men on separate sides; but more creatively they gather in couples around the main couple as a sign and pledge of their support for life.

More and more couples are dropping the whole bridesmaid/ groomsman roles and involve their families and friends in other ways in their ceremony and celebration. Expect cries of outrage if you dare to depart from the Hollywood photo op run way model—but congratulate yourself on making it your wedding—not theirs.

On anniversaries, the wise husband always forgets the past—but never the present!

Miss Manners tells us that there is no such thing as fashionably late, as you will realize if your bridegroom is not waiting at the altar when you get there.

Unless it is a surprise party, the guest of honor should be there to greet the guests.

32

Your Procession(s)

WELCOME

As Dr. Jerry Jampolski wrote: "Love means letting go of fear—and expectation—and judgment."

- Hosts welcome: Can you see that the one who welcomes everyone—to any celebration: rehearsal dinner, wedding ceremony, reception etc.—is, in fact, the host?

- This is your wedding, the bride and groom should welcome their families and friends—with welcoming gift bags for out-of-town guests—and at the beginning of all the other activities: showers, cocktail parties, and wedding rehearsal, rehearsal dinner, wedding and reception (and sometimes a closing brunch.)

- Can you imagine—even feel--the intimacy and power of a greeting from the bride and groom—as opposed to the parents or minister or DJ or coordinator?

- If this whole celebration is really something you are doing—and not something being done to or for you—then don't you owe your guests a warm welcome (as you might in your own home) and a grateful acknowledgement: "Thank you for joining us at this lovely moment. You honor us with your presence."

- If someone else is picking up the tab, then (as mentioned elsewhere) isn't it also proper for them to speak words of welcome and then turn the floor or microphone over to you—or you could welcome everyone and offer special gratitude to those whose generosity made all this possible? (Always remembering to thank your beloved partner whose love made all this worth the effort!)

- Will it help if I give you some examples of the many forms such a welcome might take?

♥ *Robert welcomed 80 guests with a love poem to his bride Sarah*:

ONE WEEK AFTER LOVE CAME TO TOWN

I have realized love at this present moment.
I feel fearless.

It's as if you've leaned the flame in your heart into my life and turned all that frightens me into ash.

I'm struggling just to think about you, because you are now a part of that which thinks.

You are running in my blood and beating in my heart.

You are a part of me so I don't have to think of you to remember you.

You are on this side of my skin, not out there, not away from me.

♥ *Brian wrote a poem to welcome everyone to his and Katie's Lake Tahoe wedding*:

THE GATHERING

Here, deep in the woods, is the place where our family gathers

A sunlit opening by the lake where only your presence matters

It is here that we laugh, we sing and we cry

It is here that our minds will wander and our emotions will let fly

It is here that the heart is found and thoughts become words

It is here that music is discovered and notes become chords

Here we will make promises that will stand the test of time

Here I will become yours and you will become mine

So, welcome our brothers and sisters, our friends and our kin

Come and sit down, we are about to begin. *(That's a welcome!)*

33

♥ *For their wedding theme "angels" Kelly and Joe had Cousin Tricia write a poetic welcome:*

Angels watch over us every night and every day

They bless our lives in very special ways

They surround us in good times and bad times alike

And though we can't see them

We never leave their sight!

For how special are we

That God granted us such a gift:

Many that guide us and give us that lift.

We are blessed by families who have loved us for years

With answered prayers that our angels be constantly near.

♥ Justin opened his wedding to Melissa with a musical welcome of Sinatra's "I've Got The World On A String…I'm In Love" and the bride sang back from the balcony "Send Me Someone To Love." (Musical welcomes only work if you can really sing—and they could!)

♥ One of my grooms who sang with a barbershop quartet—his fellow singers were his groomsmen—welcomed his surprised bride and guests with a beautiful four-part harmony barbershop ballad. Other brides and grooms have used music to welcome or to pray or to express their love for each other—very powerful, but puts a bit of pressure on you—easier to get a dear friend or very talented family member to chant your musical message.

Leslie and Paolo welcome each other and then their guests.

♥ My niece, Francie married husband Patrick with at least eight fabulous musical numbers interspersed—but all were performed by professionals—professionally accompanied. When talented singer actress, Paige got married, she sang with a choral group before the wedding—to warm up the guests—and then her groom, Steve, also a professional actor tap danced into church. Leave it to the pros!

♥ Leslie and Paolo exemplified what many brides are doing today with their "destination weddings." They spent 3-4 days before the wedding enjoying their guests with a series of low-key, homey, comfortable parties and picnics at their riverside villa, so that by wedding day, we had bonded—in fact we had become real friends. No spectators at that wedding!

34

Your Welcome

"Lord, take me where you want me to go; let me meet who you want me to meet; tell me what you want me to say, and keep me out of your way." (Favorite prayer of Fr. Mychal Judge, Franciscan Chaplain to the NYFD who died with his men on 9/11/02)

- Why readings often do not work: The main reason that most wedding readings simply do not work is that the reader does not "get out of the way." Most wedding readers are so nervous, excited and self-conscious, they call attention to themselves—and not the reading.

- Most wedding readings sound like the hurried, jittery, self-absorbed reading of a 12 year old—impossibly rushed and disastrously mindless: just a jumble of words and no idea what they are reading or how it connects to the bride and groom (readings need an introduction: why was this chosen, what does it mean…?)—and the overall message and meaning for your celebration.

- Levels: The most common levels of wedding readings are:

  1. Beginner: word after flat, lifeless word—without feeling or meaning.

  2. Intermediate: text is proclaimed slowly and seriously, with some emotion and intelligence.

  3. Advanced: the reading is prayed—reverently, dramatically, as a brilliant gift to the couple and the congregation.

- Even actors and teachers and those used to public speaking need extra preparation and direction for the very special challenge of a wedding setting. The best wedding readers are those who love the bride and groom so much that they can get over themselves—forget their own nervousness—and proclaim the reading as a prayer for and a love sonnet to the bride and groom.

Top: Francie and Patrick's readers and singers; Above: Jennifer and Harry do what few couples do: they listen to and enjoy their own wedding readings.

- Familiar: If your reading is well known and used often at weddings like Paul's Love Letter to the Corinthians, you can be fairly certain that folks have heard the words but never prayed the meaning, so it must be slowed to half speed (1-2 second pause at each punctuation mark; 2-3 second pause or full stop at every period) and powerfully presented.

- Unfamiliar: If you have chosen an unfamiliar reading like *The True Love*, then your guests will require extra time to absorb the words, internalize the meaning, and reflect on the message. It is helpful to make time (20-30 minutes) after the larger (60-90 minute) rehearsal (others may leave for the dinner celebration) so your readers can practice out loud and in the place or pulpit, with the microphones and acoustics they will need to work with at your wedding and with direction.

Your Readings and Readers

35

Top: Eber and Betsy; Above: Kendi and Bob read to each other.

- Binder for Readings: Be sure to create a simple, elegant white binder with all the readings, three-hole punched and clipped in—so that no one pulls a shabby piece of wrinkled paper out of their pocket to read at your beautiful, sacred celebration. This little "bound" collection of all your readings, prayers of the faithful, and any other material is easy to make and inexpensive. Biblical readings should be read from a real bible.

- Four short readings: My experience suggests that four short readings—perhaps two scriptural and two secular—sometimes with a musical meditation in between—are about right. But I have witnessed as many as 15 brief 30-second readings (about 12 minutes), that create a profound impression. In any case, the readings must be connected thematically—and someone (reader or celebrant) needs to point out the connection—and the connection to the bride and groom.

- Sources: Today's Internet offers so many resources to explore possible readings, you certainly do not need a sampling here. The bible is an obvious source because it has an inner power and spiritual density and impact. But don't overlook poetry, children's stories, the lyrics from meaningful songs (even as they are read, your guests will hear the melody,) special prayers or blessings or even personal compositions such as love letters or prayerful petitions from family and friends.

- Theme first: Be sure to nail down your overall theme first—and then you can begin to assemble readings and music that enhance and reinforce that focus and central message.

Sonnet 53
By Pablo Neruda

Here are the bread, the wine, the table, the house:
a man's needs, and a woman's, and a life's.
Peace whirled through and settled in this place:
the common fire burned, to make this light.

Hail to your two hands, which fly and make their white creations, the singing and the food:
salve! the wholesomeness of your busy feet; viva! the ballerina who dances with the broom.

Those rugged rivers of water and of threat, torturous pavillions of the foam, incendiary hives and reefs: today

they are this respite, your blood in mine, this path, starry and blue as the night, this never-ending simple tenderness.

Sarah and Robert chose Neruda – in English and Spanish – for their Antigua Guatemala wedding.

Your Readings & Readers

"Now you will feel no rain, for each of you will be shelter to the other. Now you will feel no cold, for each of you will be warmth to the other. Now there will be no more loneliness, for each of you will be companion to the other. Now you are two bodies, but there is only one life before you. Go now to enter into the days of your togetherness, and may your days be good and long upon the earth." (Apache Wedding Prayer)

"Father, hear our prayers for this bride and groom, who today are united in marriage before your altar. Give them your blessing and strengthen their love for each other. We ask this through Christ Our Lord. Amen." (Traditional Christian Prayer)

DAILY PRAYER OF THE MISSIONARIES OF CHARITY

Dear Jesus,

Help me to spread Thy fragrance everywhere I go. Flood my soul with Thy spirit and light. Penetrate and possess my whole being so that all my life may only be a radiance of Thine. Shine through me and be so in me that every soul I come in contact with may feel Thy presence in my soul. Let them look up and see no longer me but only Jesus. Stay with me and then I shall begin to shine as you shine, so to shine as to be a light for others.

"HELLO BROTHER"

Just a stranger on the beach
Just in sight but out of reach
Just the sand and shells to teach
Just another, "Hello Brother"

Just a stranger on the street
Just some body on two feet
Just the nerve for eyes to meet
Just another "Hello Brother"

I have nothing I would not share
With someone I thought might care
I'd even risk goodbys and go
For the chance to say, "Hello...Brother"

Just a star-warm in the cold
Just a smile and hand to hold
Just a one-upon-a told
Just another, "Hello Brother"

Just a love when life seems loss
Just a stone without the moss
Just a stranger on a cross
Just another, "Hello Brother"   *Fr. Miles Riley*

- VERTICAL DIMENSION: Prayer is usually defined as talking—or listening—to God. God as Creator, supernatural, divine, as you understand God to be. Weddings are so horizontal already—social, familial love feasts—they deserve and need a little of the vertical or transcendent dimension. You are celebrating a sacrament, a mystical covenant that is larger than life and deeper than human.

- INVITE GOD: To prepare for this book, I wrote to 55 of my favorite brides and grooms, couples I thought got it right. I asked them what they liked about their weddings, what they learned, and what they would do differently. I also asked them to include their own Ten Commandments for a great wedding—and for a great marriage. One of their strongest recommendations was: "Invite God to your wedding!"

- Your prayers are a way to invite or include God in your celebration. Not with dreary formulas but with warm, personalized invocations and benedictions. You might work on this with your minister, priest or rabbi (all experienced with praying!) to create a prayer or two—not from some prayer book, but from your heart.

On the subject of prayer, I remember the three-year-old girl whose parents had taught her the Lord's Prayer. And now she was ready for her first solo run. She did wonderfully: "Our Father, who art in heaven...." All the way to the end, which came out this way: "And lead us not into temptation but deliver us from e-mail." Clearly a daughter of our electronic, digital, internet age!

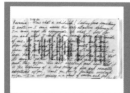

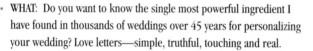

LOVE LETTERS

"How do I love thee? Let me count the ways. I love thee to the depth and breadth and height my soul can reach, when feeling out of sight for the ends of Being and ideal Grace. I love thee with the breath, smiles, tears of all my life!—and, if God choose, I shall but love thee better after death."

Elizabeth Barrett Browning

Love Letters—simple, truthful, touching and real

Your Love Letters

- **WHAT:** Do you want to know the single most powerful ingredient I have found in thousands of weddings over 45 years for personalizing your wedding? Love letters—simple, truthful, touching and real.

- **HOW:** Love letters you write to each other months before wedding day—some couples exchange and read them, some save them for the wedding, some save them for the honeymoon or their first anniversary—and you give a copy to your celebrant who is preparing you for marriage and will serve as your MC at the wedding—giving permission for appropriate excerpts to be woven into your ceremony: sometimes as readings, more often as part of your chaplain's reflections.

- **PLANNING:** Where did this idea come from? Was it 25 or 35 years ago? I only remember, as a young priest, my favorite question as we began our 6-12 months of marriage preparation was: "What one quality or characteristic most attracted you to this person? What unique value or virtue do you find most loveable?" (Thirty minutes later, I would ask them the tougher question: "What one thing would you most like to change in your partner? What about him or her is still a work in progress?")

- **REFLECTION POINTS:** But they enjoyed the first question and would enumerate the good points—except, unfortunately, they usually got it wrong and started telling me how this person made THEM feel, how the other had changed and enhanced THEIR life…Which is fine but then I would have to remind them that they were telling me about themselves—not the other person. Try to give me an x-ray profile of your loved one through your eyes and heart.

- **IMPACT:** Eventually, I hit on the Love Letter idea as a way to get them to tell me what was so special about this person they wanted to marry and grow old with. It was a powerful insight into the partner and their unique love—and I began to realize that what they were writing about each other was a thousand times more compelling and revealing than anything I could read or say—and I would beg their permission to share parts of their love letters that related to our overall theme. That would help elevate our celebration from a lovely event to a loving experience, from a familiar ritual to a personalized sacred drama.

Your LOVE LETTERS

Allow me to share a few excerpts from recent wedding love letters as examples and hopefully as inspiration for your own:

Heather and Marshall

Katie and Brian

Top: Julie and Chris; Above Leslie and Nick

Dear Marshall,

I love you for leaving Santa Barbara, your favorite place on earth and moving to cold foggy San Francisco to live closer to me. I love you for your incredible spirit and appreciation for life. I love you for your amazing ability to always make the right decisions. I love you for your patient manner and your "go with the flow" attitude. I know you will make the tough times in life seem easy. I love you for your intelligence because you were smart enough to fall in love with me.

Dear Heather,

You are truly a beautiful person inside and out. I'm sure that when people see us walking down the street together, they must think you are blind. Don't worry, I look much better after a couple of Mai Tai's. Your beauty is only surpassed by your kindness and generosity. You always put the needs of others in front of your own. Your spirit and laughter light up the room. My friends loved you immediately and they pretty much hate everyone. You will be a wonderful role model for our children— and your husband.

Dear Brian,

I continue to be amazed by all the qualities you possess and continue to grow into. You still have the same fun-loving quality and ability to make me laugh that lured me in initially. I also value your intelligence, generosity and ability to remain so non-judgmental. I think you realize that I view you as the closest thing to a human encyclopedia. You are extremely humble, supportive of your family and friends and supportive of me.

Dear Katie,

You are my sanctuary, my Shangri-La where I can retreat when life is askew. You are my North Star, my guiding point that shows me my way back to reality. You are my fountain of youth, keeping me young in heart and in spirit. You are my sun, giving me the energy I need to live and grow, while keeping my life on the correct orbit.

Your Love Letters

Your
LOVE LETTERS

40

Leslie, My Bride,

I cherish the joy and playfulness you bring to my life. You bring me peace and lightness. I admire your poise and level-headed insight. I am so proud of your understated beauty. You carry yourself with such dignity and grace. It is your grace that shines through and captivates me. I trust your opinion of people and things. More important, I trust you with my open heart.

Nick,

I knew you were special the first time I met you. I could see your eyes through your sunglasses. They were beautiful and warm. I remember your eyes and how wonderful I felt in them. I still feel that way, exactly. It's like trying to describe something that is bigger than the two of us put together, bigger than this world.

Dear Kelly,

I was nervous, scared, excited. I almost backed out. But when you walked in, I was in shock. You were even more beautiful in person than you were in a picture…Your beliefs and dreams were the same as mine…You have showed me honesty, integrity and trust. I love you with all my heart.

Dear Joey,

I want you to know how truly happy I am to be with you—and how everyday I thank God for bringing us together. I am so proud of you for who you are and what you believe in. You are an honest, loving, caring, giving person who will always do your best to make me feel happy and loved. You remind me to relax, not to be so serious all the time, and, most importantly, you make me laugh. I know that you will be a loving caring husband and one super amazing dad!

Dearest Carlito,

I so look forward to 60 years from now, when we are in our 90's, waking up by your side, feeling your warm wrinkly skin touching mine, seeing your beautiful smile, and gazing deeply into your rich blue green eyes, and remembering all the adventures we have shared…and, knowing you, you'll

Top left: Kelly and Joey; Above: Megan and Charlie

probably still have your six pack!...Your positive energy, down-to-earth personality, intellectual curiosity, sense of adventure and humor!

My Love,

I give myself to you and in doing so I promise to give you love unconditional and passionate, a life filled with laughter and new adventures and my unwavering trust, loyalty and respect…I am enthralled by your beauty and enthusiastic love for life, friends and family. I remember the smile that adorned your face as we climbed our first mountain and watching you ski like a dream…You always have an open ear for my troubles—and love for my family and friends…and are forcing me to learn patience…When we are sitting on the porch by the sea, 60 years from now, when your hair's gone from blond to white, and the lines on your face reflect the smile you have always worn, I'll still continue to look lovingly into your timeless bright blue eyes and savor every moment we had and all those to come. Heck, we are only 90 and the grandchildren just got some new kites. Let's go fly!

Dear Robert,

I love you because you taught me to say "why not" instead of "I can't", because you taught me to break some useless rules like drinking coffee, eating pizza, and relaxing on a Wednesday morning, because you taught me the beauty of listening, because you have shown me that we are inseparable from the trees and the ocean and even the bees, because you compliment me daily, because even though you think fashion magazines are poison, you will buy me one every now and then, because you do not try to change me, because you are not afraid to hang out with ladies and babies all day long, because you leave me loving post-it notes in the shower, under my pillow, wrapped around my hair dryer, in my closet and on the rear view mirror of my car, because you are one black belt ninja who can also dance, because your greatest extravagance is books, and because you open heartedly do anything for anyone in my family.

Dear Sarah, My Love,

I accept you: positive and negative, peak and valley, beauty and beast, hot and cold, fire and ice, rich and poor, love and hate, big and small, happy and sad, up and down, sinner and saint, yes and no, right and wrong, leading and following, birth and death, beginning and end, hard and soft, fast and slow, dark and light. I love you for being so elegant, having a passion for teaching, needing—not wanting—to travel, for loving your family and for holding my hand when the plane takes off.

*Top: Courtney and Mark;
Above: Bob and Kendra*

Dear Bob,

I just knew you were the one: when your beautiful blue eyes looked directly into mine when you spoke to me, when you never interrupted me while I was speaking to you—even if you had heard it all before; I just knew by your sense of humor, strength, kindness and complete sincerity, by the way you speak of your parents and brother and grandmother with love and admiration; I just knew when you said: "Go ahead and paint it any color you want."

Dear Kendra,

I laugh to myself when I think of the thoughts that went through my head every time I saw you at the store. I always admired how you could be happy and pleasant with everyone you came into contact with…I hope you realize how much love your family and friends have for you. You always put them and their needs first. Your selflessness is but one of the things I love about you…

As Kelly and Joe quoted Amy Bloom on the cover of their program:

"Marriage is not a ritual or an end. It is a long, intricate, intimate dance together and nothing matters more than your own sense of balance and your choice of partner."

41

As Dr. M. Scott Peck reminded us: "Love is a free choice of the will—which desires the spiritual growth of the loved one."

- Do you know how simple it is to create your own vows—to enhance and personalize the basic formula—and three critical points: I give me to you, I accept the gift of you, and it's forever?

May I suggest ten essential ingredients for effective vows (or any meaningful communication)—the ten P's that will make your promises sing:

- PLANNED: reflect, share with each other, dream about them, pray over them, write up several drafts and review them with your celebrant

- PERSONAL: write from your heart, not just your head

- PARTICULAR: be specific, concrete, clear—not just mushy platitudes

- PICTORAL: the language of our age is pictures and music—paint pictures

- PARABLE: most important, tell a love story—stories are all we remember

- POSITIVE: positive works better than negative ("sickness, poor, death…")

- PASTORAL: articulate your love covenant with caring compassion

- POISED: stay centered, deep within yourself—from your soul

- POWERFUL: write and speak with passion, with words of feeling

- PERSUASIVE: if you are convinced, then you will convince one another (and us!)

Here are some real life examples from brides and grooms who wrote their own vows:

Heather and Marshall wrote:

"I take you to be my wife/husband. I promise to be your biggest fan and your greatest supporter. I will express my love for you in ways both big and small. I will always try to fill your life with happiness and laughter. There will be good times and there will be tough times but my love and my commitment will remain constant. Above all I promise to be your best friend and to love you as long as I shall live."

Sarah and Robert wrote:

"I give you my love. I promise to play with you and share my life openly with you, so that we may continue to grow and laugh together. To say yes to the joys and sorrows of the world, and travel with you through the adventures of life. And from this day on, to dance to the Music and give thanks to the Musician."

Charlie vowed:

"I give myself to you and promise to give you my love unconditional and passionate, a life filled with laughter and new adventures and my unwavering trust, loyalty and respect."

Megan responded:

"Charlie, as my best friend and partner for life, I promise with my whole heart to love you unconditionally and affectionately; I promise to trust you while respecting and admiring your individuality; I promise to enlighten your days with laughter and continue to seek new adventures together; with these promises I will challenge us to grow closer and help each other strive to become better human beings each and every day."

Ranny and Bob wrote:

"The meaning of marriage begins in the giving of words. We cannot join ourselves to one another without giving our word. And this must be an unconditional giving, for in joining ourselves to one another we join ourselves to the unknown…In the world we are never given two known results to choose between, but only one result that we choose without knowing what it is." "So we now commit ourselves to one another, and before God, family and friends, declare our intention to be wife/husband to him/her, to speak the truth in love, to treat one another with respect and encourage each one's fulfillment through all the circumstances that life may bring."

Ranny and Bob

Melissa and Justin summed their vows up:

"I will love you forever—no matter what."

Sample vows to choose from:

- I acknowledge you as my spiritual partner here to teach me about love.

- I promise to support you, to be all that you can be.

- I intend to learn about love every day; how to give love, receive love, and serve love.

- I will share my heart and body with you; including fears and joy as they arise.

- I vow to celebrate your body in all its changing forms.

- I promise to seek support in time of need.

- I promise to keep our agreements

- I vow to be faithful in my spiritual path and to support you in yours

- I let go of all that holds me back from loving you

- I pledge myself entirely to this path of marriage

43

Everything about your wedding should symbolize unity: from the proposal and engagement, to the showers, to the parties, to the gifts to the announcements and invitations and your web page, to the actual celebration of the wedding weekend—and beyond! It's all about oneness, covenant, commitment, and two becoming one—for a lifetime!

The conscious, aware bride spots opportunities to highlight and reinforce that oneness in her own special unique ways:

- VOWS: words of unity

- RINGS: signs and promise of unity and extra special when all are invited to bless

- UNITY CANDLE: tapers lit by parents are used to light the one unity candle

- SAND: as many as eight different colors can be poured into a clear vase—each symbolizing different people or aspects—and then mixed together, as one

- LASSO, VELA, MONEDAS OR ARRAS: powerful Latino reminders of two becoming one

- Jewish chupah or Orthodox rug: both indicate loving support and togetherness

- Your wedding party: showing loving support

- FLOWERS: as gifts to your mothers and/or Jesus' mom at the side alter.

- MUSIC: a brilliant, non-verbal sign of oneness of heart—with or without lyrics—but most moving when sung by the whole assembly (like at birthdays and New Year's)

- PRAYING TOGETHER: even a simple Our Father galvanizes the congregation

- A COMMUNAL PEACE GREETING: initiated by bride and groom—and shared by all

- COMMUNION: when your faith allows and extra meaningful when given by the couple

- FINAL OR NUPTIAL BLESSING: tremendous symbol of unity when shared with all present

- TAKING HIS FAMILY NAME—or he taking yours (some grooms tell me they like hers better!)

- YOUR RECEPTION: when it is a continuation of the sacred drama and not just another party (check again Chapter 3: the difference between an event and an experience)

- Guest book or signing a large photo of the bride and groom (although I don't know what they do with it afterwards—hang it over the fireplace?) perhaps best are the instamatic individual photos of each guest signed by them and tucked in your wedding scrapbook.

- YOUR HOSPITALITY or "working the room" (most couples take dance lessons when they might better take hospitality lessons)

- TOASTS BY PARENTS—enough of the chauvinistic sexism: moms have had equal rights for generations—the bride worries: "Mom might cry"…Great! Truly amazing weddings have tears and laughter!

- TOASTS BY YOUR MAID OF HONOR AND BEST MAN: can be real symbols and inspiration for unity—but usually need coaching and some gentle nudging from you to set the tone!

- SHARING FOOD AND DRINK: unfortunately, it's just a meal unless given some real direction and the correct musical background

- DANCING: on balance, this may be one of the best symbols of unity at your entire wedding!

Top: Kelly and Joe light their unity candle

Your Symbols of Unity

America is the great "melting pot"—even if melting and merging slowly. If either you or your groom enjoy family roots or cultural connection outside our beloved USA, please incorporate that into your ceremony and weekend celebration. We all learn from this and we love it!

- ASIAN: Debra married Rich both as his American bride escorted down the aisle by her mom and dad—and as his Chinese bride in cultural bridal gown. In wardrobe, location, foods and language the wedding was wonderfully bi-cultural.

- AFRICAN: When Brenda married Gordie in Cabo, Mexico, it was important to include customs and language from Mexico, as well as Gordie's African American traditions: such as "jumping the broom" where godmother places a decorated broom in the aisle and the couple literally jumps over it as they start their new life together. Other African wedding customs include: pouring water over a plant to represent the continuation of life, lighting the kinara which holds seven tapers, tasting foods that remind one of the sweet and the bitter in life and love, or the shoe ceremony where you give each other a new pair of shoes to signify your "new walk" in life.

- FRENCH: Chris and Larry got married in Les Beaux, southern France, so as they exited the 12th Century church, locals provided a flowered archway and then danced with the bride and groom around the town square.

- ITALIAN: American bride Leslie and Italian groom Paolo used flags to signify their international, intercultural merger, as well as bilingual programs reading "You give me your sky, I give you my ocean" and T-shirts with their theme: "Forti Insieme" (Strong together!) When Ranny (Francesca) married Bob (Roberto) in Positano, all the townspeople came out to wish them well—"Viva La Sposa!"—as they processed through the streets from church to reception.

- RUSSIAN: Ukrainian Michelle married New Zealander Robert on a mat or carpet hand-embroidered by loving relatives as a symbolic reminder of their continued support.

- JEWISH: It was important to Catholic Carol to marry Jewish Steven beneath a lovely chupah—silk veil on four columns—as a sign of heavenly and familial protection.

- SCOTTISH: When marathon runners, Libby and Ian married, they expressed their cultural merger on the cover of their program with both of their family shields, and more dramatically with Ian's (and his father's and best man's) Scottish kilts….(Only appropriate with handsome legs!)

Top: Debra in her Chinese wedding dress with Rich

- HAWAIIAN ? POLONYSIAN?: Hawaiian weddings are easy to inculturate because they are both American and international, Pacific Island culture and still USA. So, when Sherry married Doyle in Kona, they followed the Hawaiian tradition by exchanging leis and a kiss at the very beginning of the ceremony—Hawaiians don't wait until the end!

- LATIN: Many Latin cultures celebrate the corda, a large figure eight rosary, lovingly crafted by grandma and often reverently placed over the heads of the bride and groom by their baptismal godparents. Joy and Brett created a magnificent variation: they bought a fresh water pearl for each of their guests, attached the pearls to long beige cords with which they had me tie their hands together as a symbol of oneness, after exchanging vows and rings, and then surprised their guests by presenting each with his or her own single pear necklace to remember the moment and stay connected. As I often pray at the close of the wedding: "Thank you for coming to the wedding—please stay for the marriage."

- HISPANIC: Another age old Hispanic tradition is the arras or monedas where the bride and groom hand one another 13 gold coins, representing Christ and the 12 apostles, as a sign and promise that they will continue to take care of one another. Megan and Charlie came up with a lovely variation by naming each of the 13 gold coins for their favorite virtues—and then presented each of their 140 guests in Puerto Vallarta with a single gold coin and virtue to take home.

46

Top left: Ian and father and best man putting best Scottish foot forward

Left: Bride Jennifer and Bridesmaids in Indian gowns.

- INDIAN: Other brides also celebrate the multicultural global village that is the glory of America. Jennifer married Michael in both Indian and American wedding attire.

- HOLD THE RICE! The one symbol that does not belong is the rice throw. Rice is food for half the people in the world—besides, potatoes or carrots would be easier to clean up. Years ago, rice was replaced by birdseed (which is slippery, especially for seniors on pavement or steps) which was replaced by helium balloons (lovely symbols which eventually must come down to pollute the environment) which were replaced by confetti (colorful and less damaging but still messy) which was replaced by soap bubbles. How about showering the newly weds with smiles, cheers, hugs and love?

- INVOLVE MOM: Ah, finally, a chance for your mother (and father) to make a real contribution (whether they are paying for it or not.) They have held and attended many more dinner parties (or buffets or barbecues or pot lucks) than you. Here's where you can put their experience and expertise to good use—and make them feel really needed (they are!)

- PARTICULARS: There are so many elements in a dinner or luncheon for 50-250 people: choice of venue, catering, food and beverage selection, color scheme, floral arrangements, place cards, seating plan, and on and on. Let mom be your partner/producer to track the myriad minutiae—don't burden yourself or burn yourself out on the little stuff. You and your groom, as principal hosts, have far more important priorities. Let mom worry about additional costs not included in the price quote: like sales tax, gratuities and overtime fees; she can track the written contracts with all services provided— and arrange to pay with credit cards for your protection.

- YOUR DECISIONS: Because you know your friends best, you two can decide on the spirit of the affair (overall feel, indoors or outdoors, midday or evening) and you two decide on the music both during the meal and for dancing afterward, you decide whether to have a bar (open bar or no bar) you decide how to position yourselves: (with your bridal party or with your families—this is a family love feast).

- YOUR MAIN JOB: Your main job is to meet and greet, to work the room, to thank everyone for coming and give them a chance to hug the bride which is the main reason they came in the first place: hoping that a little of your love light, your glow, spiritual luminosity, your aura would rub off on them.

Top: Katie and Brian's creative first dance.

Left: Jennifer's Dad offered his farm for the reception.

Left: Paige and Steven trip the Light Fantastic!

Left: Sharon Rose and Joe transformed her family's backyard into a garden reception for 125 guests.

47

- THANK YOU NOTES: Many modern brides send out thank you notes as gifts come in—a few super-organizers have their thank you notes mailed before the wedding—but, whatever your situation, you might at least review your list of gifts received so you can thank a few folks in person at your reception. And will that impress them! Of course, you still need to send a written grateful acknowledgement after the honeymoon.

- TRADITIONS: Every culture has its own unwritten rules about things like: blessings (ask your celebrant, if he or she has joined you for the meal) toasts (allow for very few and keep them short and sweet,) first dances (not just your Fred and Ginger moment, but a lovely way to share the dance floor with your new parents-in-law and other relatives,) garters and bouquets (as brides get more mature these old empty customs seem to be disappearing—to the disappointment of older aunts,) or cake cutting and sharing (it is not cute or kind to smash cake in your new spouse's face)

- CAUTION: Today's brides and their families are also conscious and conscientious about avoiding drunk driving—by providing caring transportation alternatives. Helping your guests get home or back to their hotels is an integral part of your hospitality.

- TIMING YOUR EXIT: Forty-five years ago, most brides and grooms left their reception for the honeymoon before the end of the evening—thereby unfortunately missing much of the celebration and, even more unfortunately, making it clear that they were the stars rather than the hosts of this party. Nowadays, most couples not only remain to say goodnight and goodbye to their guests, but then stay somewhere nearby so they can join the morning-after brunch: to share some wonderful stories and memories with loved ones..

Top left: Hope and Tony were able to entertain all their guests in her grandmother's backyard.

Left: Tiv and Gerv giggle with bride's Mom at her backyard reception.

Left: Louise and Jeff transformed their parish gym into a ballroom!

Left: Katie and Brian enjoyed their reception at his parent's lakeside home.

Favors the perfect way to reinforce your theme: inexpensive, imaginative—with a dash of humor.

Here are a few examples to trigger your own imagination:

- In general: inscribed rocks, shells and sand dollars, flower leis, glass or silver hearts, baseball caps with your logo, candles, chocolates, bells, angel statues, herbal sachets, pretty soap packets, cookies, jams, monogrammed match books, laminated prayer cards, frisbees and anything but those tired fertility almonds.

- In particular: a number of brides put each guest's name and table number in a beautiful silver picture frame, which guests keep as a gift.

- Adrianne and Phil, at their very spiritual wedding, gave everyone a laminated prayer card.

- Alex and John, at their roaring 20's wedding, gave everyone a long pearl necklace with this note: "Wear these pearls loose or tight and feel the magic of the night."

- Louise and golf pro hubby Jeff, gave everyone an inscribed golf ball as a table favor.

- Hope and Tony, wishing every guest love and luck, gave them Lotto scratchers—hopefully.

- Carol and Steven gave everyone an etched silver yo-yo as a reminder that life has ups and downs—and the importance of playfulness.

- Whitney and Chris, in keeping with their thoroughbred Kentucky horse motif, had 8 inch chocolate horses at each place. (Yummy!)

- Lauren and Ian, who own five cocker spaniels together, gave all their female guests silver necklaces in the shape of a cocker and all the male guests silver cocker cuff links—and all 70 guests received rubber flip flops for the beach celebration.

- Tracey and Robert, knowing that their wedding would be a scorcher, printed their program and words of thank you on the back of a large and useful fan.

- Sharon and Joe, for their backyard bash, brewed their own beer and reinforced their garden theme by giving everyone a packet of sweet pea seeds—to keep growing.

- Katie and Brian emphasized their cooking together theme by giving all 320 guests a small personalized bottle of delicious olive oil.

- Gayle and Patrick, who used 8 different colors of sand mixed together as their symbol of unity, gave every guest a tiny plastic baggie filled with their ceremonial sand.

- Megan and Charlie, married in Mexico, turned the traditional arras or monedas—13 gold coins representing Christ and the 12 apostles—from symbolic dowry into a gift for all 140 guests; and asked each guest to bring to their wedding some symbol of their love and best wishes: a beautiful, participated "second collection."

- Miriam and Owen, fly fishing fanatics who married in Cape Cod by the sea, gave everyone a day of fly fishing lessons the day after (and their priest got a rod and reel.)

- Rebecca and Mark had a friend take separate photos of each guest as they arrived and then brilliantly highlighted their family togetherness theme by having each guest during the meal write a prayer or blessing on a square of fabric, which the groom's mom could then sew into a marriage quilt.

- Melissa and Jason, who hand crafted most of their wedding materials, created 17 elegant hammered copper flutes which stood on wrought iron tripods and held a cornucopia of spectacular flowers on each table at their reception—and then gave each of their wedding party and close family one of the flutes to remember them by: like the wedding, a labor of love.

- Joy and Bret, as their symbol of wedded unity, made a gorgeous three foot rope out of 50 strands of brown cord with a fresh water pearl at the end of each; they used the rope to bind their hands together after their exchange of vows and rings—and then, later during the dinner, separated the strands and presented each of their 50 guests with their own pearl necklace as a reminder of our celebration of oneness, beauty and love.

50

Check out these web sites for other ideas:
www.beau-coup.com
www.orientaltrading.com
www.myownlabels.com
www.islandweddingshop.com
www.idofoundation.org

- And my personal favorite: Courtney and Chad placed a card at each seat: "A donation has been made in your honor to: Operation Smiles: free reconstructive surgery for thousands of children in developing countries; and also Challenged Athletes Foundation: for people with physical disabilities who want to compete athletically." (What a gift of love!)

"May your joys be as bright as the morning, and your sorrows merely be shadows that fade in the sunlight of love. May you have enough happiness to keep you sweet, enough trials to keep you strong, enough sorrow to keep you human, enough hope to keep you happy, enough failure to keep you humble, enough success to keep you eager, enough friends to give you comfort, enough faith and courage in yourself to banish sadness, enough wealth to meet your needs, and one more thing: enough determination to make each day a more wonderful day than the one before."
(An Irish Toast)

- The best toasts are love stories or stories of love. Great toasts involve lyrical language, a few involve profound insight, and the most enjoyable involve humor—since laughter is the closest distance between people. But, in every case, the key to a successful toast is specificity, colorful, concrete details and descriptions.

- Tell stories, because that's how human beings communicate! You will find other tips for powerful communication in Chapter 32 on writing your own vows. Love stories, because affection and admiration work better and last longer than "roasts" or cynical put-downs.

- Examples probably work best. Dear Abby's favorite wedding toast suggests three phrases that guarantee a happy marriage: "I was wrong." "You were right." "I love you."

- At Katie and Brian's wedding, their favorite family toast was offered: "The Four Hinges of Hell: You steal, you lie, you swear, and you drink. But when you steal, you steal away from all that is evil. When you lie, you lie in the arms of the one you love. When you swear, you swear by your country and your God. And, when you drink, you drink with me to the happiness of our bride and groom."

- I can't remember who offered this toast: "May you love deeply, laugh heartily, practice patience, and smile often. May you dream together, grow, be crazy, give, give in, and trust enough to take. May you see many sunrises, listen to the rain, and savor special moments. May you rediscover each other, listen carefully, and always have open hearts."

- Someone else suggested these seven simple rules for happiness and wholeness: Wake up, Dress up, Shut up, Stand up, Look up, Reach up, and Lift up!

- When Meghan married Danny, her father gave a simple toast that captured everyone's attention. The bride remembered it this way. "My dad's toast has stuck with us. He's an avid reader and created an analogy comparing his only daughter to a favorite book. My wedding was the final chapter and he didn't want it to end—as you don't want a good book to end … but, he was looking forward to reading the sequel—my life with my husband."

Top: father Jerry toasts his "Rose"
Left: Meghan and Dan applaud the toasts

Your Toasts

• At Colleen's wedding to Rob, her dad, Maury gave the toast he has given at all four of his six children's weddings: "It takes many people to raise children. Judy and I have always surrounded our children with the kind of people we want them to be, so thank you all for being those people." Maury has since embellished that splendid toast with this wisdom: "Be as loud a voice in the lives of your kids as any other kid on the block. Give them a sense of their past as well as their future. We replaced the tradition of tying tin cans to the departing vehicle by attaching a priceless gift: the values you would have them take with them on their journey." And remember the wise words of a chief executive whose many years of selfless service were primarily responsible for the success of his mega corporation: "Yesterday, I took a young lady to the altar on my arm who was a total stranger to me. That's what it cost me to achieve the success I have had in the company."

• And mother Judy offered this blessing or good housekeeping seal of approval: "Marriage, what a mystery. How can we pledge the rest of our lives to one person, how do we know if it is the right one, what will life bring us as a couple, will we be able to blend our two families together, will our religious beliefs be sacred to us and our children, will our partner become a better person as we grow and change in this marriage? Now that they are all happily married, I can say without exception that LOVE IS NOT BLIND and they all exhibit deep love and tenderness toward one another."

• When Miriam married Owen her polyglot father toasted the bride and groom in Gaelic, German, French and English—wishing all their guests welcome and God's blessings for health and life for the bride and groom. Powerful—in every language—especially the language of the heart!

• Megan and Charlie are kite-surfers and extreme skiers and fabulous athletes, so at their Puerto Vallarta wedding, Charlie's brother and best man Dutch gave this toast: "I was only 14 months old the day Charlie was born, but even I could tell he was an accident waiting to happen. By the time he was 7, he's had more stitches than most professional hockey teams. As a child he had some irrational fear about hurting his hands, so that whenever he'd trip, he'd throw his hands behind him and let his head take the brunt of the fall. The scars on his forehead ended up looking like some hopeless game of tic-tac-toe. That's why he wears his hair long in front. Even today, when Charlie goes skiing the local medical teams go on high-alert— especially if the ski trip involves lighting a gas stove. But Charlie finding Megan was no accident. It's obvious to anyone who knows them that they were born to be together. And I know they'll have a long and happy life together, and no matter where they go, Megan needs to know the fastest route to the emergency room."

• And, finally, excerpts from the father of the bride, Dr. Mike: "Heather has been the ideal daughter. I did not say perfect. She did a few little things growing up, like most kids do. Like the times she borrowed her mother's convertible and went cruising—way before she had her learner's permit! Or the numerous times she hosted large teenage gatherings at our home—while we were away. We have forgiven her these things….Heather's friends call her "Triple Booked" in reference to her endless energy and her willingness to do things that need to be done. When Heather really wants something, she finds a way to get it. Marshall, that is not a warning but a compliment…. Marshall is a special guy. He has the keenest intuition of anyone I have met. At times I feel him read my head better than an MRI. He is kind and considerate and best of all he is very, very nice to our little girl. They are perfect for each other and have all the fundamentals: happiness, respect and love. To Heather and Marshall: May you always be as happy as Sandee and I. May you look back in 30 years and realize that you love each other more than you did on your wedding day. Cheers.".

Top: Debbie and Peter enjoy the toasts.

"Love has nothing to do with what you are expecting to get—only what you are expecting to give—which is everything. What you will receive in return varies. But really has no connection with what you give. You give because you love and cannot help giving. If you are very lucky, you may get loved back. That is delicious, but it does not necessarily happen."
(Katharine Hepburn)

- One bride groaned recently: "$1000 for a cake? Heavens, it's only flour and eggs!" She knows it's a lot more than that—but she's right: one more item the bridal big biz inflates because they know they can. They write with a heavy pencil because the bride's piggy bank is supposedly bottomless.

- If you really like cake, and really want a cake, invest not merely money but also imagination and creativity. My niece, Francie, whose whole theme image was the deeply spiritual sand dollar (one glued on every program, another as table marker and another as place setting) naturally ordered a cake with sugar sand dollars circling each layer. Regrettably but humorously, the baker misunderstood and served a gorgeous white bridal cake—adorned with silver dollars!

- For those who are really into cake, how about the fun addition of a groom's cake, typically a dark chocolate or fruit cake? For example, Sydney ordered a yummy chocolate piano for her piano-playing doctor groom, Scott; and Marisa came up with a huge, delicious guitar cake for her musician groom, Brian. Boxed slices of the groom's cake can be offered as take-home favors for your guests.

Top left: Sydney's and Scott's bridal cake and Groom's cake; Right: Alicia and Darren's tiered cake; Bottom left: Marisa's groom's cake for Brian.

- Most brides serve the wedding cake as dessert for their sit down dinner. More and more seem to be skipping the "anniversary cake" or top layer of the wedding cake—which often in the past was taken home and stored in the freezer to accompany the champagne and wedding video or photo album on your anniversaries.

- Many brides today order a smaller sized and less expensive cake to be put on display and then have their caterer serve the majority of guests from a large sheet cake in the kitchen. I've never heard a word of complaint and suspect most guests don't even notice—or care. If you do decide on a baker for your cake, be sure to enjoy taste samples and ask to see photos of bridal cakes they have created in the past.

Your
CAKE

- Cakes are, of course, optional and some brides choose another sweet or dessert which they (and many of their guests) enjoy a lot more. Like ice cream—my personal favorite—which Katie and Brian served to their 320 guests, possibly because the groom's father owned Dreyers Ice Cream. In fact, Libby and Ian aren't that fond of cake, so they served hot fudge Sundays. Carol and Steven offered cheesecake and lollipops. Hope and Tony provided cakes, cookies and other individual desserts—all baked by Hope's mom. Chris and Larry, married in France, followed the French tradition and ordered a fabulous profiterole pyramid. Whitney and Chris, married in the Blue Grass state, and in keeping with their theme of thoroughbreds, gave every guest a magnificent chocolate horse—bigger than this book! The deeper symbolism is sweets for the sweet—not cake. Hooray!

54

Left: Kisses sweeter than cake! Right: Lisa and Chris's cake in the Napa vineyard.

Top left: Kelly and Joe; Above Jenny and Michael

- For more creative cake ideas, check out www.wilton.com for insights into choosing, transporting, cutting and freezing your cake—plus recipes, if you are ambitious enough to bake your own cake (or have a heroic mom!) Another imaginative alternative is www.elegantcheesecakes.com for tiered and lovely wedding cakes that can be shipped almost anywhere. And, for you brides who love chocolate, www.thechocolateguy.com will rent you a chocolate fondue fountain, turning dessert into a hands-on adventure for all!

Count on a few surprises on your wedding weekend. And, like the wedding itself, how you handle those surprises will make all the difference—for everyone.

For example, Kara wanted her beloved St. Bernard, Nino Von Bernetta to serve as the "Flower Hound" at her wedding to Adam. (I had to convince the local pastor that Nino was a baptized Catholic to let him into church.) Nino came in draped with garlands of flowers and two flower girls and two ring bearers and at the most solemn moment of their wedding, Nino broke wind—and a little boy in the first pew announced the fact to the entire church in a loud voice. When everyone stopped laughing, I whispered to the bride and groom: "You have your wedding memory!" (Word to the wise: pets and kids can be in your procession, then seated discreetly.)

- Emily surprised Craig by wearing the most outrageous bloomers with big red hearts all over them, so that when he knelt to reverently remove the garter…well, you get the picture!

- Harry surprised Jennifer—as many thoughtful, loving grooms do on wedding day—with a tender love note, a little gift, and this message: "I'll be waiting for you at the altar."

- Francie and Patrick got their surprise from the baker who misread the instructions: "every layer is surrounded by sand dollars" (their theme) and instead they got silver dollars. Yikes!

- David surprised Patricia and her Latin American family by singing "Besame Mucho" at the reception.

- Melissa and Justin surprised everyone with a musical opening to their ceremony: he sang "I've Got the World on a String" and she sang back "Send Me Someone to Love." For a moment, no one was quite sure if it was a wedding or a musical.

- Music is a powerful message. Music and pictures are the language of our age. But they must be used creatively and professionally. (You have to be able to sing—well!) Many Irish couples or Scottish couples—Libby and Ian were both—will arrange for bagpipes to close the ceremony or, like Sharon Rose and Joseph, to lead guests from the church to the reception. Just as Latin couples—or couples married in Mexico, like Kristie and Drew or Brenda and Gordie or Megan and Charlie or Christine and Mo—arrange for a mariachi band to surprise their guests and send chills up their spines.

- Kelly and Ron surprised everyone by having swimming suits under their wedding garments and leading the wedding party into the lake at their reception in 103° summer heat.

- At Michelle and Eric's wedding on the 4th of July, two surprise symbols were hidden behind the altar: an American flag and a volley ball, since they met on the court.

- Miriam and Owen surprised everyone at their Cape Cod wedding by arriving at the reception by yacht—and then the day after, the bride and groom, both avid fly fishermen, flew in famous Lou Tabory to give everyone who wished a day long, hands-on lesson in fly fishing.

- One adorable little ring bearer surprised the entire congregation by growling his way—slowly, from side to side, hands clawed—down the main aisle of church. When his embarrassed mother demanded: "What do you think you're doing?" he replied innocently: "Trying to be the ring bear!"

- Welcome these surprises: they underline our human vulnerability and add a dash of spice to your wedding. Long after you have forgotten everything that went smoothly, you'll remember the surprises and thank God. ∞

Top: Kelly, Ron and the entire wedding party
take a surprise swim at their reception

"Lord, grant me the courage to change what I can, the patience to accept what I cannot change, and the wisdom to know the difference." The Serenity Prayer

- Unlike surprises, crises are real emergencies that test your mettle, your calm under pressure, your cool and your class—and, sometimes, even your faith.

- By crisis, I mean more than inconvenient, upsetting, unplanned accidents: like members of your wedding party getting drunk at your rehearsal dinner and making inappropriate remarks or passing out during your wedding. We once had a hung over bridesmaid pass out and gash her head open on a marble pillar; I rushed to the pulpit and asked: "Is there a doctor in the church?" Fortunately, there were three!

- By crisis, I don't mean those silly pranks which some ill-advised friends and even family members think will be cute or funny; nor am I referring to mishaps like glass table tops or punch bowls shattering and sending shards of broken glass into the buffet; nor do I refer to more serious accidents like folks falling on slippery steps or a slippery dance floor.

- By crisis, I mean something much more serious than old boy friends or wedding crashers who come to disturb the peace and must be dealt with kindly and firmly; even more serious than manipulative, take-over vendors-from-hell who confuse coordination with control and professional with pushy.

- By crisis, I mean a terrible, interruptive, potentially catastrophic event that threatens your wedding or those you love or even you. Let me give you two very different examples from my experience—hoping that you will never have to face either—a serious accident and a last minute cancellation.

- Thank God that the accident happened to Patrice and Michael because they and their amazing families were able to handle it. We were at Old St. Mary's Church, which many of you know since it is half way down one of San Francisco's steepest streets at the entrance to China Town. Just as the balcony choir was about to start the processional, we heard a series of loud crashes out in the street. The brakes had released on a huge truck which then careened down the hill, hitting cars, a bus stop, another car and finally came to rest crushed into the side of the limo carrying the bride and her father. The blow knocked the driver from the limo, dented the stretch limo like a coke can and pinned the bride and her dad in the back seat. I ran to them and they were able to get the window open but not the door. The groom managed to crawl through the window to comfort his bride to be. Our groomsmen rushed from the church to the most serious injury: the truck had banged a car into a woman up against a cement wall across the street and trapped her husband under the car. The groomsmen literally lifted the car off the man and freed his wife. As soon as fire trucks and ambulances began to arrive to care for the cut and bruised and badly shaken, I gave the bride and groom 10 minutes to gather their wits and went back into church to explain to our 400 upset and unnerved guests what had happened and asked that they join me in a spontaneous prayer of gratitude that no one had been killed and the bride and father were being helped out of the crushed limo and would join us momentarily. As I tried to calm our congregation, I remembered that the bride and groom had chosen as their wedding theme many months earlier: "Laughter and Love." Of course, there was nothing funny about this tragedy—but there was plenty of heroic, loving support!

After the ceremony, the fleet of motorized cable cars the bride had arranged for stood empty while our 400 guests chose to walk (safely) up the hill to a beautiful dinner, fun toasts, and much music, which gradually enabled everyone to slip into a celebratory mood. The next morning, waiting at SFO for their honeymoon flight, Patrice and Michael caught a glimpse of the morning newspaper and immediately called me at the parish. "Father, thanks again for your wonderful celebration yesterday and for helping with our crisis. Have you seen the morning paper yet? No…well, check it out, because a photo of the accident, the story, and our "wedding memory" as you called it is on the front page." Priests are trained to handle crises—brides are not! The message is not that an old padre stayed cool under fire—but that a young bride and groom displayed presence, caring, and smoothly, maturely wove the totally unexpected into the fabric of their love celebration.

Patrice and Michael stayed calm in their crisis.

- The other unthinkable crisis that sometimes arises is a last minute cancellation of the wedding. In my experience, quite a few have been called off within weeks of the date, several at or just after the rehearsal, three or four the day of the wedding. Perhaps, the most awkward was the time the doorbell rang just as I was on my way over to church. There stood the bride and groom and best man. I said: "I'll be right there." They replied: "No, actually, we have something to tell you." I said: "Please, come right in." They stepped inside the front door of the rectory and announced: "We've decided not to go through with it." I asked if the people in the church—or at least their families—had been told. No, they answered, no one—we thought you could explain it to everyone. Half joking, I tried to wiggle out: "The textbooks suggest that the best man should make the announcement." "No way," he responded.

So I grabbed the bride's and groom's hands, marched across the courtyard and the three of us walked up the center aisle together. On the altar, we turned around and I addressed a mystified congregation: "Folks, we have good news—and even better news. The good news is that the bride and groom love each other enough to realize that they should not get married today." The crowd gasped in shock, the mothers swooned, some giggled and some cried. "The even better news," I just adlibbed on the run, "is that we are still going to have a reception! Let's party!" (I figured all was paid for at the country club—why not enjoy.) No, to answer your question, I did not go to the "party" and have no idea whether they ever did get married.

- As difficult a crisis—emotionally, psychologically, financially— as a last minute cancellation can be, it's a lesser crisis than divorce.

HONEYMOON

"Whoever is happy will make others happy too."

(Anne Frank)

Top left: Ranny and Bob married and honeymooned in Postitano, Italy;
Left: Sarah and Robert married and honeymooned in Guatemala;
Right: Sherry and Doyle married and honeymooned in Hawaii.

The father of the bride in Babylon 4000 years ago supplied his new son-in-law with all the mead or honey beer he could drink in a month; this period was called the Honey Month—and later the Honeymoon.

- Consult a travel agent for advice on honeymoon locations off season--better prices, flights and rooms

- Pick a place not too far away—a week to 10 days will refresh you

- Treat yourselves to a comfortable wedding night suite nearby with all the honeymoon extras, pop in on friends and family at brunch, and then depart for your honeymoon.

Here are some internet sites to facilitate your honeymoon planning:

- www.honeymoonlocation.com even offers packing tips—don't forget to pack a surprise gift for your new hubby.

- www.visitmexico.com features local experts on the best sights, hotels and restaurants from Cancun to La Paz

- www.gocaribbean.com details the unique characteristics of 36 Caribbean destinations, including Aruba's 42 major dive sites and Martinique's Parisian atmosphere

- www.cruise.com lists many voyages from nearly 100 cruise lines with sailing dates, itineraries and prices

- www.gorp.com will provide creative options for domestic adventure travel—from national parks and forests to secluded campsites

- www.honeyluna.com allows you to register your honeymoon, as do www.aruba.com and www.weddingchannel.com

- www.orbitz.com enables you to plug in your desired destination and price—and the Deal Detector sends you an email when the fare drops to your level

- www.epinions.com and www.igougo.com and www.tripadvisor.com all enable you to check out various places from folks who actually stayed there

- www.xe.com offers all the out-of-country money exchange rates

- www.airlinemeals.net gives you the scoop on meals in the air—complete with photos and passenger reviews—sorted by airline

- www.travelzoo.com features a Top 20 email newsletter with the best travel bargains

- www.shermanstravel.com screens the best deals and reviews destinations

- www.matrix.itasoftware.com displays every published airfare, even for smaller airlines

- www.idofoundation.org allocates 5% of your trip for charity—how lovely and loving!

Entering their honeymoon hotel, a young bride whispered to her new husband: "Let's pretend we've been married a long time." "All right," he replied. "Do you think you can carry both suitcases?"

May I wish you, "Happy Honeymoon!".

58

"Thank you for coming to the wedding—please stay for the marriage!" My favorite closing line, after asking God's blessing on the newly weds and all couples present.

- Your wedding lasts an extraordinary weekend; my wish for you is a marriage that lasts a lifetime.

- Your wedding costs thousands; remember your marriage is priceless.

- Your wedding touches the lives and loves of several hundred people; however your marriage touches the family, the community and the world.

Top right: Alicia, Darren and family;
Bottom left: Kara, Adam and family; Bottom right: Shannon, Fulty and family.

The following is some advice from my favorite couples on how to have a great marriage in six key categories:

COMMITMENT
  Be faithful
  Work at it
  Fall in love with the same person every day
  It's not about you
  Keep a united front with others

TIME TOGETHER
  Have a date night every week—especially after you have kids
  Take annual mini vacations with and away from each other
  Find a personal hobby that gets you out one night a week
  Be best friends
  Remember why you got married

APPRECIATION
  Say I love you everyday—and mean it
  Express your gratitude to and for one another
  Be each other's head cheerleader
  Brag about your spouse to others—especially to family
  People change, and the point of marriage is to grow together

COMMUNICATION
  Listen, trust, play, and write notes
  Manage your finances wisely and openly
  Honesty, intimacy, equality
  Fight fair, in the present and in the first person "I"—and naked (it won't last as long!)
  Say "I'm sorry" and "Thank you"
  Have sacred time to be with each other and sacred space (one room) just for love

60

SPIRITUAL WELLNESS

Invite God into your marriage

Create spiritual connections

Take care of yourself—no one else can make you happy

The only person you can change is you

Volunteer to serve others

COPING WITH CRISIS

Know that you are strong enough to make your marriage what you want

Share your pain

Forgive

Expect hard times—all marriages endure difficult times

Keep it simple—don't complicate your lives

Top: Kelly, Ron and family; Left: Sheri, Bobby and family; Right top: Olivia, Gervee and girls; Right bottom: Erin, Joe and family.

Clockwise from top left: Debra and Rich's family; Sienna, Peter and family; Lisa, Chris and family, Mark and Courtney's son, Jack! – The End!

"Men and women are so different the amazing thing is that we can even talk to each other."

Sigmund Freud

According to Buddha and my Spiritual Director, "Life is difficult," (and, once you realize that it is difficult, it is not so difficult at all.)

This practical guide-book for personal weddings is dedicated to the over 2000 couples who have honored and blessed me for 50 years by allowing me to help them prepare for the awesome sacrament of marriage and witness their wedding vows and share in their celebrations of faith and family, life and love!

All these couples have given me the precious gift—an amazing grace—of participating in one of the most sacred moments in their lives. Many have invited me back to baptize their children, counsel their families, and even formally say good bye ("God be with you") to deceased loved ones.

One of the 55 couples I asked to share their wedding stories and wisdom was Chris and Larry Reese. Chrissy ran a child care center in our parish and was a dear friend for many years. She made me promise, if she ever found the right guy, that I would marry them in southern France where she had studied in college. It worked out that the year they chose I was teaching in Rome and could hop over to Provence, southern France (Vincent van Gogh country) where she and Larry were wed.

Chris and Larry Reese marry in the south of France.

I wrote to Chris and Larry, thousands of miles away and 15-20 years after their magical celebration, and they agreed to contribute. They sent me many pictures and 10 pages of single-spaced, typed, email memorabilia and reflections. Because books are like babies, they take 9 months to be born, before we could birth this baby, Chrissy lost her fight with cancer, and returned to God. Larry gave me permission to dedicate it to her—and them—and their creative "Love Story."

The Author & Acknowledgments

ABOUT THE AUTHOR:

Miles O'Brien Riley grew up with talented parents and six creative brothers and sisters. Their priorities were family and faith. He entered St. Joseph's College Seminary in 1952, studied Philosophy at St. Patrick's Seminary and Stanford, and four years of Theology at the Gregorian University in Rome where he was ordained a priest in 1963. He later

completed a PhD in communications at the University of California in Berkley and the masters program in Marriage and Family Counseling at the University of San Francisco. He swears that his favorite and fastest hours of the day were working with couples: preparing them for marriage--or helping them enrich their love and stay married.

Fr. Miles' 45 years of ministry included pastoral service in seven parishes and over 25 years as director of communication for the Archdiocese of San Francisco. He has written and directed five musical comedies, published 12 books, hundreds of articles and reviews. He has produced a dozen films and hosted over 1500 television and 4000 radio programs, receiving 3 Emmys, 10 National Gabriel Awards, and 4 Proclaim Awards for outstanding mass media production. He has conducted communication training workshops throughout the United States and in 50 countries worldwide. He is listed in Who's Who in Religion in the U.S., Who's Who in the Catholic Church in the U.S., Who's Who in America and Who's Who in the World. Now retired from active ministry, he's working on humility.

Special thanks and blessings to:

- Bobbie Frohman who lovingly and creatively produced the one hour audio CD version of "It's Your Wedding, Not Theirs;"

- Patti Appel who devoted her artistic genius to every aspect of design and layout, bringing brilliant beauty to every page;

- Mary Knippel, copywriter extraordinaire, who toned my prose and toned down my anger at the wedding industry;

- Maureen Golden of Author House who saw the book's potential — when other publishers hesitated to challenge the powerful wedding industry— and helped us reach out to tomorrow's brides;

- The 55 couples I asked to share their wedding wisdom in retrospect: as they look back 10, 20, 30 years later, what worked and what would they do differently? Your practical insights will hopefully enlighten others;

- The over 2000 couples over the last 45 years who honored me with a request to help them prepare for and celebrate their weddings —an awesome responsibility and a sacred trust—you welcomed me into your homes and hearts.